CEOE Field 24
OSAT
Middle Level English
Teacher Certification Exam

By: Sharon Wynne, M.S
Southern Connecticut State University

XAMonline, INC.
Boston

Copyright © 2007 XAMonline, Inc.
All rights reserved. No part of the material protected by this copyright notice may be reproduced or utilized in any form or by any means, electronic or mechanical, including photocopying, recording or by any information storage and retrievable system, without written permission from the copyright holder.

To obtain permission(s) to use the material from this work for any purpose including workshops or seminars, please submit a written request to:

XAMonline, Inc.
21 Orient Ave.
Melrose, MA 02176
Toll Free 1-800-509-4128
Email: info@xamonline.com
Web www.xamonline.com
Fax: 1-781-662-9268

Library of Congress Cataloging-in-Publication Data

Wynne, Sharon A.
 OSAT Middle Level English Field 24: Teacher Certification / Sharon A. Wynne. -2nd ed.
 ISBN 978-1-58197-787-5
 1. OSAT Middle Level English Field 24.   2. Study Guides.   3. CEOE
 4. Teachers' Certification & Licensure.   5. Careers

Disclaimer:
The opinions expressed in this publication are the sole works of XAMonline and were created independently from the National Education Association, Educational Testing Service, or any State Department of Education, National Evaluation Systems or other testing affiliates.

Between the time of publication and printing, state specific standards as well as testing formats and website information may change that is not included in part or in whole within this product. Sample test questions are developed by XAMonline and reflect similar content as on real tests; however, they are not former tests. XAMonline assembles content that aligns with state standards but makes no claims nor guarantees teacher candidates a passing score. Numerical scores are determined by testing companies such as NES or ETS and then are compared with individual state standards. A passing score varies from state to state.

Printed in the United States of America œ-1

CEOE: OSAT Middle Level English Field 24
ISBN: 978-1-58197-787-5

TEACHER CERTIFICATION STUDY GUIDE

Table of Contents

DOMAIN I.   **LISTENING AND SPEAKING**

COMPETENCY 1.0 UNDERSTAND LISTENING AND SPEAKING FOR INFORMATION AND UNDERSTANDING 1

Skill 1.1   Identify techniques for organizing information for formal presentations 1

Skill 1.2   Analyze factors affecting a listener's or viewer's ability to understand spoken language in different contexts 2

Skill 1.3   Distinguish among styles of language appropriate to various purposes, content, audiences, and occasions 3

Skill 1.4   Evaluate the use of visual materials for an oral presentation 5

COMPETENCY 2.0 UNDERSTAND LISTENING AND SPEAKING FOR LITERARY RESPONSE AND EXPRESSION, PERSONAL APPRECIATION, AND ENTERTAINMENT 6

Skill 2.1   Judge the effectiveness or appropriateness of given details or examples for making a presentation or a performance more interesting or appealing 6

Skill 2.2   Recognize the different roles of voice and intonation patterns in oral presentations of stories, poetry, and drama 8

COMPETENCY 3.0 UNDERSTAND LISTENING AND SPEAKING FOR CRITICAL ANALYSIS, EVALUATION, AND PERSUASION 10

Skill 3.1   Identify appropriate strategies of organization and delivery in relation to given content, audience, purpose, and occasion 10

Skill 3.2   Analyze the role of critical thinking skills in effective listening, speaking, and viewing 11

Skill 3.3   Recognize the role of body language, gestures, and visual aids in communicating a point of view 11

COMPETENCY 4.0 UNDERSTAND LISTENING AND SPEAKING FOR SOCIAL INTERACTION IN A VARIETY OF FORMAL AND INFORMAL SITUATIONS 13

Skill 4.1 Demonstrate knowledge of effective listening and speaking in conversation 13

Skill 4.2 Examine techniques of effective listening and speaking in small- and large-group situations 14

Skill 4.3 Analyze factors affecting listening and speaking in various social contexts 15

TEACHER CERTIFICATION STUDY GUIDE

| DOMAIN II. | WRITING |

COMPETENCY 5.0 UNDERSTAND WRITING FOR INFORMATION AND UNDERSTANDING 16

Skill 5.1 Evaluate information from various sources for use in a research project... 16

Skill 5.2 Revise drafts to improve their effectiveness 16

Skill 5.3 Apply skills for presenting and organizing content in informational writing 20

COMPETENCY 6.0 UNDERSTAND WRITING FOR PERSONAL EXPRESSION AND SOCIAL INTERACTION 21

Skill 6.1 Demonstrate awareness of connotation and figurative meaning in selecting language for a given expressive purpose 21

Skill 6.2 Judge alternative introductory or concluding sentences for a personal essay on a given theme 22

Skill 6.3 Analyze problems relating to the effectiveness of narrative or descriptive materials and identify appropriate revisions 24

Skill 6.4 Apply strategies for composing personal texts 26

COMPETENCY 7.0 UNDERSTAND WRITING FOR CRITICAL ANALYSIS, EVALUATION, AND PERSUASION 27

Skill 7.1 Analyze the organization of an editorial or argumentative essay on a given topic 27

Skill 7.2 Distinguish reasons, examples, or details that support a given argument or opinion... 28

Skill 7.3 Apply strategies for developing and evaluating persuasive writing.... 29

TEACHER CERTIFICATION STUDY GUIDE

COMPETENCY 8.0 UNDERSTAND HOW TO USE THE WRITING PROCESS TO DEVELOP AND REFINE WRITTEN TEXTS 31

Skill 8.1 Apply strategies for generating ideas before writing 31

Skill 8.2 Demonstrate knowledge of procedures for drafting written texts 35

Skill 8.3 Apply strategies for revising and editing written materials 36

COMPETENCY 9.0 EDIT WRITTEN TEXTS TO ACHIEVE CLARITY, UNITY, AND EFFECTIVE ORGANIZATION 37

Skill 9.1 Revise sentences to eliminate wordiness, ambiguity, and redundancy 37

Skill 9.2 Revise sentences and passages to subordinate ideas, maintain parallel form, and connect related ideas 38

Skill 9.3 Solve problems related to text organization 39

Skill 9.4 Use descriptive language and varied sentence structure to enhance writing 39

COMPETENCY 10.0 APPLY KNOWLEDGE OF STANDARD ENGLISH GRAMMAR, USAGE, AND MECHANICS 40

Skill 10.1 Revise syntactic errors in a text 40

Skill 10.2 Revise misplaced or dangling modifiers 41

Skill 10.3 Revise nonstandard capitalization, punctuation, and spelling 42

TEACHER CERTIFICATION STUDY GUIDE

DOMAIN III. READING

COMPETENCY 11.0 APPLY SKILLS FOR READING FOR INFORMATION AND UNDERSTANDING 48

Skill 11.1 Identify and apply distinctions between general statements and specific details 48

Skill 11.2 Draw conclusions from a given passage or visual message 49

Skill 11.3 Infer information from a given passage or visual message 49

Skill 11.4 Summarize information in a given passage or visual message 50

COMPETENCY 12.0 APPLY SKILLS FOR READING FOR LITERARY RESPONSE AND PERSONAL ENJOYMENT 51

Skill 12.1 Analyze an author's use of figurative language to convey ideas, sensory impressions, or emotional effects 51

Skill 12.2 Interpret the use of rhythm, rhyme, or imagery to evoke a response in the reader 52

Skill 12.3 Analyze the use of language to portray character, develop plot, or create a mood in a given passage 53

COMPETENCY 13.0 APPLY SKILLS FOR READING AND VIEWING FOR CRITICAL ANALYSIS AND EVALUATION 55

Skill 13.1 Distinguish between fact and opinion in a written or visual message 55

Skill 13.2 Judge the relevance, importance, or sufficiency of facts or examples in a writer's argument 56

Skill 13.3 Assess the objectivity or credibility of various sources of information 57

Skill 13.4 Determine how an author uses tone and style to present a particular point of view 58

TEACHER CERTIFICATION STUDY GUIDE

COMPETENCY 14.0 UNDERSTAND THE USE OF READING STRATEGIES AND METACOGNITIVE TECHNIQUES TO CONSTRUCT MEANING AND AID COMPREHENSION 60

Skill 14.1 Demonstrate knowledge of strategies to use before reading to enhance comprehension 60

Skill 14.2 Demonstrate knowledge of strategies to use during reading to enhance comprehension 60

Skill 14.3 Distinguish different levels of comprehension 61

Skill 14.4 Analyze strategies used to determine word meanings 62

TEACHER CERTIFICATION STUDY GUIDE

DOMAIN IV.   LITERATURE

COMPETENCY 15.0 UNDERSTAND GENRES OF FICTION AND DRAMA AND THEIR CHARACTERISTIC FEATURES 63

Skill 15.1 Analyze elements of fiction in passage context 63

Skill 15.2 Compare the characteristics of types of fictional narratives 67

Skill 15.3 Demonstrate knowledge of types of drama and their characteristics 68

Skill 15.4 Analyze elements of drama in context 69

COMPETENCY 16.0 UNDERSTAND GENRES OF NONFICTION AND THEIR CHARACTERISTIC FEATURES 70

Skill 16.1 Compare and contrast characteristics of types of nonfiction 70

Skill 16.2 Apply criteria for evaluating nonfiction works of various genres 71

Skill 16.3 Analyze elements of nonfiction in context 72

COMPETENCY 17.0 UNDERSTAND FORMS OF POETRY AND THEIR CHARACTERISTIC FEATURES 74

Skill 17.1 Analyze the formal characteristics and distinctive content of narrative poetry 74

Skill 17.2 Relate various types of lyric poetry to their formal characteristics 79

Skill 17.3 Analyze elements of poetry in context 81

COMPETENCY 18.0 UNDERSTAND THE SOCIAL AND CULTURAL ASPECTS OF LITERATURE, INCLUDING THE WAYS IN WHICH LITERARY WORKS AND MOVEMENTS BOTH REFLECT AND SHAPE CULTURE AND HISTORY 86

Skill 18.1 Apply knowledge of the characteristics and significance of mythology and folk literature 86

Skill 18.2 Analyze the expression of cultural values and ideas through literature 88

Skill 18.3 Analyze the role of given authors and works in influencing public opinion about and understanding of social issues 89

MIDDLE LEVEL ENGLISH

COMPETENCY 19.0 UNDERSTAND CLASSIC AND CONTEMPORARY LITERATURE FOR YOUNG ADOLESCENTS 91

Skill 19.1 Demonstrate knowledge of characteristics of writers, works, and genres of literature for young adolescents 91

Skill 19.2 Analyze in passage context major thematic elements associated with adolescent literature 93

Skill 19.3 Examine ways in which adolescent readers gain insights into themselves and others through literature 94

Skill 19.4 Identify criteria for selecting literature for young adolescents 97

COMPETENCY 20.0 UNDERSTAND MAJOR THEMES, CHARACTERISTICS, TRENDS, WRITERS, AND WORKS IN AMERICAN, BRITISH, AND WORLD LITERATURE 100

Skill 20.1 Examine the role of major writers, works, and movements in the development of American, British, and world literature 100

Skill 20.2 Analyze in passage context significant themes and genres in American, British, and world literature 115

Skill 20.3 Recognize major characteristics and themes of multicultural literature written in the United States 120

DOMAIN V. LANGUAGE AND INTERDISCIPLINARY LANGUAGE ARTS

COMPETENCY 21.0 UNDERSTAND THE HISTORICAL, SOCIAL, CULTURAL, AND TECHNOLOGICAL INFLUENCES SHAPING THE ENGLISH LANGUAGE 124

Skill 21.1 Analyze the significance of historical events that have influenced the development of the English language... 124

Skill 21.2 Relate English derivatives and borrowings, including slang terms, to their origins in other languages 134

Skill 21.3 Analyze regional and social variations in language in the United States 135

COMPETENCY 22.0 UNDERSTAND FUNDAMENTAL CONCEPTS RELATING TO THE STRUCTURE, ACQUISITION, USE, AND ANALYSIS OF LANGUAGE 136

Skill 22.1 Distinguish structural features of languages 136

Skill 22.2 Apply principles of language acquisition and use 136

COMPETENCY 23.0 UNDERSTAND THE INTERRELATIONSHIP OF LANGUAGE ARTS SKILLS AND THEIR INTEGRATION WITHIN OTHER CONTENT AREAS 140

Skill 23.1 Recognize the ways in which reading, writing, listening, and speaking interrelate and mutually influence one another................... 140

Skill 23.2 Analyze methods of integrating language modes to promote learning... 140

Skill 23.3 Apply techniques and activities for integrating the language arts with other content areas 141

Sample Test.. 142

Answer Key 158

Answers with Rationales.. 159

TEACHER CERTIFICATION STUDY GUIDE

Great Study and Testing Tips!

What to study in order to prepare for the subject assessments is the focus of this study guide but equally important is *how* you study.

You can increase your chances of truly mastering the information by taking some simple, but effective steps.

Study Tips:

1. Some foods aid the learning process. Foods such as milk, nuts, seeds, rice, and oats help your study efforts by releasing natural memory enhancers called CCKs (*cholecystokinin*) composed of *tryptophan*, *choline*, and *phenylalanine*. All of these chemicals enhance the neurotransmitters associated with memory. Before studying, try a light, protein-rich meal of eggs, turkey, and fish. All of these foods release the memory enhancing chemicals. The better the connections, the more you comprehend.

Likewise, before you take a test, stick to a light snack of energy boosting and relaxing foods. A glass of milk, a piece of fruit, or some peanuts all release various memory-boosting chemicals and help you to relax and focus on the subject at hand.

2. Learn to take great notes. A by-product of our modern culture is that we have grown accustomed to getting our information in short doses (i.e. TV news sound bites or USA Today style newspaper articles.)

Consequently, we've subconsciously trained ourselves to assimilate information better in neat little packages. If your notes are scrawled all over the paper, it fragments the flow of the information. Strive for clarity. Newspapers use a standard format to achieve clarity. Your notes can be much clearer through use of proper formatting. A very effective format is called the *"Cornell Method."*

> Take a sheet of loose-leaf lined notebook paper and draw a line all the way down the paper about 1-2" from the left-hand edge.
>
> Draw another line across the width of the paper about 1-2" up from the bottom. Repeat this process on the reverse side of the page.

Look at the highly effective result. You have ample room for notes, a left hand margin for special emphasis items or inserting supplementary data from the textbook, a large area at the bottom for a brief summary, and a little rectangular space for just about anything you want.

MIDDLE LEVEL ENGLISH

3. **Get the concept then the details.** Too often we focus on the details and don't gather an understanding of the concept. However, if you simply memorize only dates, places, or names, you may well miss the whole point of the subject.

A key way to understand things is to put them in your own words. If you are working from a textbook, automatically summarize each paragraph in your mind. If you are outlining text, don't simply copy the author's words.

Rephrase them in your own words. You remember your own thoughts and words much better than someone else's, and subconsciously tend to associate the important details to the core concepts.

4. **Ask Why?** Pull apart written material paragraph by paragraph and don't forget the captions under the illustrations.

Example: If the heading is "Stream Erosion", flip it around to read "Why do streams erode?" Then answer the questions.

If you train your mind to think in a series of questions and answers, not only will you learn more, but it also helps to lessen the test anxiety because you are used to answering questions.

5. **Read for reinforcement and future needs.** Even if you only have 10 minutes, put your notes or a book in your hand. Your mind is similar to a computer; you have to input data in order to have it processed. *By reading, you are creating the neural connections for future retrieval.* The more times you read something, the more you reinforce the learning of ideas.

Even if you don't fully understand something on the first pass, *your mind stores much of the material for later recall.*

6. **Relax to learn so go into exile.** Our bodies respond to an inner clock called biorhythms. Burning the midnight oil works well for some people, but not everyone.

If possible, set aside a particular place to study that is free of distractions. Shut off the television, cell phone, and pager and exile your friends and family during your study period.

If you really are bothered by silence, try background music. Light classical music at a low volume has been shown to aid in concentration over other types. Music that evokes pleasant emotions without lyrics is highly suggested. Try just about anything by Mozart. It relaxes you.

TEACHER CERTIFICATION STUDY GUIDE

7. **Use arrows not highlighters**. At best, it's difficult to read a page full of yellow, pink, blue, and green streaks. Try staring at a neon sign for a while and you'll soon see that the horde of colors obscure the message.

A quick note, a brief dash of color, an underline, and an arrow pointing to a particular passage is much clearer than a horde of highlighted words.

8. **Budget your study time**. Although you shouldn't ignore any of the material, *allocate your available study time in the same ratio that topics may appear on the test.*

Testing Tips:

1. Get smart, play dumb. Don't read anything into the question. Don't make an assumption that the test writer is looking for something else than what is asked. Stick to the question as written and don't read extra things into it.

2. Read the question and all the choices *twice* before answering the question. You may miss something by not carefully reading, and then re-reading both the question and the answers.

If you really don't have a clue as to the right answer, leave it blank on the first time through. Go on to the other questions, as they may provide a clue as to how to answer the skipped questions.

If later on, you still can't answer the skipped ones . . . **Guess.** The only penalty for guessing is that you *might* get it wrong. Only one thing is certain; if you don't put anything down, you will get it wrong!

3. Turn the question into a statement. Look at the way the questions are worded. The syntax of the question usually provides a clue. Does it seem more familiar as a statement rather than as a question? Does it sound strange?

By turning a question into a statement, you may be able to spot if an answer sounds right, and it may also trigger memories of material you have read.

4. Look for hidden clues. It's actually very difficult to compose multiple-foil (choice) questions without giving away part of the answer in the options presented.

In most multiple-choice questions you can often readily eliminate one or two of the potential answers. This leaves you with only two real possibilities and automatically your odds go to Fifty-Fifty for very little work.

5. Trust your instincts. For every fact that you have read, you subconsciously retain something of that knowledge. On questions that you aren't really certain about, go with your basic instincts. **Your first impression on how to answer a question is usually correct.**

6. Mark your answers directly on the test booklet. Don't bother trying to fill in the optical scan sheet on the first pass through the test.

Just be very careful not to miss-mark your answers when you eventually transcribe them to the scan sheet.

7. Watch the clock! You have a set amount of time to answer the questions. Don't get bogged down trying to answer a single question at the expense of 10 questions you can more readily answer.

DOMAIN I.   **LISTENING AND SPEAKING**

COMPETENCY 1.0 UNDERSTAND LISTENING AND SPEAKING FOR INFORMATION AND UNDERSTANDING

Skill 1.1   **Analyzing techniques for selecting and organizing information for oral presentations.**

Preparing to speak on a topic should be seen as a process that has stages: **Discovery**, **Organization**, and **Editing**.

Discovery: There are many possible sources for the information that will be used to create an oral presentation. The first step in the discovery process is to settle on a topic or subject. Answer the question, What is the speech going to be about? For example, the topic or subject could be immigration. In the discovery stage, one's own knowledge, experience, and beliefs should be the first source, and notes should be taken as the speaker probes this source. The second source can very well be interviews with friends and possibly experts. The third source will be research: what has been written or said publicly on this topic. This stage can get out of hand very quickly, so a plan for the collecting of source information should be well-organized with time limits set for each part.

Organization: At this point, several decisions need to be made. The first is what the *purpose* of the speech is. Does the speaker want to persuade the audience to believe something or to act on something, or does the speaker simply want to present information that the audience might not have? Once that decision is made, a thesis should be developed. What point does the speaker want to make? And what are the points that will support that point? And in what order will those points be arranged? Introductions and conclusions should be written last. The purpose of the introduction is to draw the audience into the topic. The purpose of the conclusion is to polish off the speech, making sure the thesis is clear, reinforcing the thesis, or summarizing the points that have been made.

Editing: This is the most important stage in preparing a speech. Once decisions have been made in the discovery and organization stages, it's good to allow time to let the speech rest for awhile and to go back to it with "fresh eyes." Objectivity is extremely important, and the speaker should be willing to make drastic changes if they are needed. It's difficult to turn loose of one's own composition, but good speech-makers are able to do that. On the other hand, this can also get out of hand, and it should be limited. The speaker must recognize that at some point, the decisions must be made, the die must be cast, commitment to the speech as it stands must be made if the speaker is to deliver the message with conviction.

The concept of recursiveness is very useful to one who writes speeches. That is, everything must be written at the outset with full knowledge that it can be changed, and the willingness to go backward, even to the discovery stage, is what makes a good speech-writer.

MIDDLE LEVEL ENGLISH

Skill 1.2   Analyze factors affecting a listener's or viewer's ability to understand spoken language in different contexts.

The more information a speaker has about an audience, the more likely he/she is to communicate effectively with them. Several factors figure into the speaker/audience equation: age, ethnic background, educational level, knowledge of the subject, and interest in the subject.

Speaking about computers to senior citizens who have, at best, rudimentary knowledge about the way computers work must take that into account. Perhaps handing out a glossary would be useful for this audience. Speaking to first-graders about computers presents its own challenges. On the other hand, the average high-school student has more experience with computers than most adults and that should be taken into account. Speaking to a room full of computer systems engineers requires a rather thorough understanding of the jargon related to the field.

In considering the age of the audience, it's best not to make assumptions. The gathering of senior citizens might include retired systems engineers or people who have made their livings using computers, so research about the audience is important. It might not be wise to assume that high-school students have a certain level of understanding, either.

With an audience that is primarily Hispanic with varying levels of competence in English, the speaker is obligated to adjust the presentation to fit that audience. The same would be true when the audience is composed of people who may have been in the country for a long time but whose families speak their first language at home. Black English presents its own peculiarities, and if the audience is composed primarily of African-Americans whose contacts in the larger community are not great, some efforts need to be made to acquaint oneself with the specific peculiarities of the community those listeners come from.

It's unwise to "speak down" to an audience; they will almost certainly be insulted. On the other hand, speaking to an audience of college graduates will require different skills than speaking to an audience of people who have never attended college.

Finally, has the audience come because of an interest in the topic or because they have been influenced or forced to come to the presentation? If the audience comes with an interest in the subject already, efforts to motivate or draw them into the discussion might not be needed. On the other hand, if the speaker knows the audience does not have a high level of interest in the topic, it would be wise to use devices to draw them into it, to motivate them to listen.

Skill 1.3 **Distinguish among styles of language appropriate to various purposes, content, audiences, and occasions.**

Slang comes about for many reasons: Amelioration is an important one that results often in euphemisms. Examples are "passed away" for dying; "senior citizens" for old people. Some usages have become so embedded in the language that their sources are long-forgotten. For example, "fame" originally meant rumor. Some words that were originally intended as euphemisms such as "mentally retarded" and "moron" to avoid using "idiot" have themselves become pejorative.

Slang is lower in prestige than Standard English; tends to first appear in the language of groups with low status; is often taboo and unlikely to be used by people of high status; tends to displace conventional terms, either as a shorthand or as a defense against perceptions associated with the conventional term.

Informal and formal language is a distinction made on the basis of the occasion as well as the audience. At a "formal" occasion, for example, a meeting of executives or of government officials, even conversational exchanges are likely to be more formal. A cocktail party or a golf game are examples where the language is likely to be informal. Formal language uses fewer or no contractions, less slang, longer sentences, and more organization in longer segments.

Speeches delivered to executives, college professors, government officials, etc., are likely to be formal. Speeches made to fellow employees are likely to be informal. Sermons tend to be formal; Bible lessons will tend to be informal.

Jargon is a specialized vocabulary. It may be the vocabulary peculiar to a particular industry such as computers or of a field such as religion. It may also be the vocabulary of a social group. Black English is a good example. A Hardee's ad has two young men on the streets of Philadelphia discussing the merits of one of their sandwiches, and bylines are required so others may understand what they're saying. A whole vocabulary that has even developed its own dictionaries is the jargon of bloggers. The speaker must be knowledgeable about and sensitive to the jargon peculiar to the particular audience. That may require some research and some vocabulary development on the speaker's part.

Technical language is a form of jargon. It is usually specific to an industry, profession, or field of study. Sensitivity to the language familiar to the particular audience is important.

Regionalisms are those usages that are peculiar to a particular part of the country. A good example is the second person plural pronoun: you. Because the plural is the same as the singular, various parts of the country have developed their own solutions to be sure that they are understood when they are speaking to more than one "you." In the South, "you-all" or "y'all" is common. In the Northeast, one often hears "youse." In some areas of the Middlewest, "you'ns" can be heard.

Vocabulary also varies from region to region. A small stream is a "creek" in some regions but "crick" in some. In Boston, soft drinks are generically called "tonic," but it becomes "soda" in other parts of the northeast. It is "liqueur" in Canada, and "pop" when you get very far west of New York.

Oral use of communication forms

Different from the basic writing forms of discourse is the art of debating, discussion, and conversation. The ability to use language and logic to convince the audience to accept your reasoning and to side with you is an art. This form of writing/speaking is extremely confined/structured, logically sequenced, with supporting reasons and evidence. At its best, it is the highest form of propaganda. A position statement, evidence, reason, evaluation and refutation are integral parts of this writing schema.

Interviewing provides opportunities for students to apply expository and informative communication. It teaches them how to structure questions to evoke fact-filled responses. Compiling the information from an interview into a biographical essay or speech helps students to list, sort, and arrange details in an orderly fashion.

Speeches that encourage them to describe persons, places, or events in their own lives or oral interpretations of literature help them sense the creativity and effort used by professional writers.

Useful resources

>Price, Brent - *Basic Composition Activities Kit* - provides practical suggestions and student guide sheets for use in the development of student writing.

>Simmons, John S., R.E. Shafer, and Gail B. West. (1976). *Decisions About The Teaching of English - "Advertising, or Buy It, You'll Like It."* Allyn & Bacon.

Additional resources may be found in the library, social studies, economic, debate and journalism textbooks and locally published newspapers.

Skill 1.4 Evaluate the use of visual materials for an oral presentation.

Tips for using print media and visual aids

- Use pictures over words whenever possible.
- Present one key point per visual.
- Use no more than 3-4 colors per visual to avoid clutter and confusion.
- Use contrasting colors such as dark blue and bright yellow.
- Use a maximum of 25-35 numbers per visual aid.
- Use bullets instead of paragraphs when possible.
- Make sure it is student-centered, not media-centered. Delivery is just as important as the media presented.

Tips for using film and television

- Study programs in advance.
- Obtain supplementary materials such as printed transcripts of the narrative or study guides.
- Provide your students with background information, explain unfamiliar concepts, and anticipate outcomes.
- Assign outside readings based on their viewing.
- Ask cuing questions.
- Watch along with students.
- Observe students' reactions.
- Follow up viewing with discussions and related activities.

COMPETENCY 2.0 UNDERSTAND LISTENING AND SPEAKING FOR LITERARY RESPONSE AND EXPRESSION, PERSONAL APPRECIATION, AND ENTERTAINMENT

Skill 2.1 Judge the effectiveness or appropriateness of given details or examples for making a presentation or a performance more interesting or appealing.

Helping students to discover what types of details or examples will enhance a particular presentation or performance will depend in good part on the assignment/s given. Possibilities for in-class performances are:

- live skits or one-act plays based on original student work
- live skits, plays or recitations based on literary texts assigned for class reading and discussion
- audio or video recordings of either of the above, e.g., a "radio play" based on Shirley Jackson's story "The Lottery."
- informative reports
- demonstration speeches, e.g., "how to make a dirt cake"
- persuasive speeches
- panel debates on course-related topics

Before assigning presentation or performance work, teachers should familiarize students with several examples of successful speeches, presentations, drama, etc. For instance, if a teacher shows the class a video recording of Martin Luther King's 1963 "I Have a Dream" speech, the teacher should first provide students with written copies of it, then ask them to do the following:

- List all written works and songs mentioned by King.
- List all historical events and persons mentioned by King.
- List all landforms and American place names mentioned by King.
- Make a list of all the metaphors and similes used in the speech.
- Make a list of words, phrases, and ideas repeated in the speech.

Next have the students, singly or in groups, evaluate and analyze all of the above. Typical questions to ask are:

- Why do you think King uses imagery from the natural world—islands, sweltering summer, etc.—to describe abstractions such as freedom, equality, justice, and injustice? Do you think that his use of metaphors shows any patterns or conscious intentions? Do you find his imagery effective? Why or why not?
- Why do you think King mentions so many landforms and American place names?
- What is the relationship to King's subject of the works and songs mentioned in his speech?
- What is the effect of King's use of repetition in the speech?

- What words would you use to describe the tone and effect of King's speech?
- How do any of the matters above relate to King's intended audience? Who is his intended audience?
- Do the contents of "I Have a Dream" offer any hints or suggestions about what to put into speeches and/or presentations in general?

A similar set of questions and exercises can apply when evaluating and analyzing a wide variety of well-known speeches, performances, and writings. The content and methods of such an approach are equally relevant and helpful to students as they prepare their own presentations. In addition, numerous speeches are available in both print (online) and video. A few of them are:

- Barbara Bush: Commencement Address at Wellesley College, June, 1990.
- Elizabeth Glaser: "Aids Speech" at the Democratic Party Convention, July 14, 1992.
- Adolf Hitler: Closing Address at National Socialist Party Congress (Nuremberg Rally), 1934.

Once a presentation or performance has been assigned, and the topics chosen, have students prepare by doing the following:

- Conduct research in the library and online to determine what others have done with the same topic and/or similar assignments.
- Consider who the audience is, then determine the appropriate tone, vocabulary, and content to get one's key points across.
- If advocating a particular cause, opinion, and/or course of action, the speaker must determine what type of support will strengthen their case (see below). He or she will also need to take into account any opposing views and determine a strategy to address and counter them.
- Take into consideration matters regarding personal delivery: what to wear, the importance of eye contact with one's audience, body language (gestures, facial expressions), and the need to avoid mumbling, speaking in a monotone or too fast.

A variety of supporting material is needed to make a successful presentation. Options for a persuasive speech, for instance, include:

- Facts, figures, and statistics
- Quotations from experts or other authoritative sources
- Quotations from literary works or news media
- Personal experience and anecdotes

The above information can be enhanced by presenting it through:

- Photographs, charts, graphs
- Video or audio recordings
- Printed handouts
- Reciting passages from a given work

For other types of speeches or presentations, have students determine what methods, support, and props are appropriate to achieve the effect they desire to have on their audience (see all of the above).

Skill 2.2 **Recognize the different roles of voice and intonation patterns in oral presentations of stories, poetry, and drama.**

Shifting into a new character calls for an analysis of that character's ways of talking, moving, and relating to others in the world. Everything a student does to give themselves the appearance—both physically and emotionally—of a character, involves an interpretation of that character's motivations, intentions and passions. Characterization is the basic decisions a student makes regarding the why and how of his or her character. They may justify their decisions based on details they notice in illustration or word, on understanding they have about similar characters in real life, and on their own motivations and intentions.

Basic frame sentence for character analysis:
"Since my character is _____, then he/she would act like _____."

This may result in a student employing a goofy, clumsy shuffle when acting in their role, or addressing everyone as "baby." The student must evolve from a child into an actor, and finally, into a specific character. It is your job to facilitate this transformation.

Child > Actor > Character

To further the immersion in their role, encourage students to call each other by their characters' names. Emphasize the "as if" nature of a play, in which the students treat characters as if they were real, with real emotions and motivations driving them to act the way they do. Do not give students your own interpretation of a character's personality. Let them create their own interpretation, and follow along with their reading of the character.

Vocal Techniques

Voice is perhaps the most important tool of interpretation in classroom theater. It can portray anger, sadness, jealousy, happiness, fear and excitement. Vocal techniques integrate word choice, emphasis, and attitude, accentuating or deemphasizing them as the student sees fit. The voice puts life into the words of the play, with intonation, pitch, loudness or softness and even accent reflecting or obscuring the intent of the speaker.

Just look at the phrase, "It's all right," as an example of the impact of voice and tone. Said with a soothing voice, it implies patience and understanding. Said with a sarcastic, cynical voice, it gives off a dismissive feeling. A host of a party might say the same phrase with suppressed frustration to a guest who has broken a favorite vase. In each case, the vocal choices made either highlight or shadow the inner thoughts of the speaker.

Encourage students to try on different vocal roles. Explain to students that while you must use the words in the script, *how* you say them is up to individual interpretation. A simple explanation is to simply tell them to "read something and then say it in your own way." Have students decide on words they want to stress by highlighting or underlining them in their scripts. Circle words that should be spoken louder and draw a line lightly through words that should be whispered. Allow students to transform vocal inflection to match with their vision of their character. They will soon combine their own attitudes and analyses with attitudinal hints the text supplies to create an effective emotional portrayal.

Storytelling Techniques

- It's important to try to have complete silence before you begin, so that the students are concentrating and focused on the story and the person reading it. Turn off any background music.
- Make eye contact with everyone. At least you should be able to see all the students from where you are sitting or standing. Move them around if necessary.
- Make sure that there are no distractions behind you – stand in front of a wall, not an interesting bookshelf or a window.
- Think about yourself telling a favorite anecdote to your friends. "Did I tell you about the time when I…" How do you tell it? What gestures and effects do you use? At what points are you sure of getting a laugh? What are you doing with your body language and how are you telling the story? Is there a particular pause before the punch-line that works wonders? Apply your style to the story you're telling.

COMPETENCY 3.0 UNDERSTAND LISTENING AND SPEAKING FOR CRITICAL ANALYSIS, EVALUATION, AND PERSUASION

Skill 3.1 Identify appropriate strategies of organization and delivery in relation to given content, audience, purpose, and occasion.

The content in material to be presented orally plays a big role in how it is organized and delivered. For example, a literary analysis or a book report will be organized inductively, laying out the details and then presenting a conclusion, which will usually be what the author's purpose, message, and intent are. If the analysis is focusing on multiple layers in a story, that will probably follow the preliminary conclusion. On the other hand, keeping in mind that the speaker will want to keep the audience's attention, if the content has to do with difficult-to-follow facts and statistics, slides (or PowerPoint) may be used as a guide to the presentation, and the speaker will intersperse interesting anecdotes, jokes, or humor from time to time so the listeners don't fall asleep.

It's also important to take the consistency of the audience into account when organizing a presentation. If the audience can be counted on to have a high level of interest in what is being presented, little would need to be done in the way of organizing and presenting to hold interest. On the other hand, if many of those in the audience are there because they have to be, or if the level of interest can be counted on not to be very high, something like a PowerPoint presentation can be very helpful. Also the lead-in and introduction need to be structured not only to be entertaining and interest-grabbing, it should create an interest in the topic. If the audience members are senior citizens, it's important to keep the presentation lively and to be careful not to "speak down" to them. Carefully written introductions aimed specifically at this audience will go a long way to attract their interest in the topic.

No speaker should stand up to make a presentation if the purpose has not been carefully determined ahead of time. If the speaker is not focused on the purpose, the audience will quickly lose interest. As to organizing for a particular purpose, some of the decisions to be made are where it will occur in the presentation—beginning, middle, or end—and whether displaying the purpose on a chart, PowerPoint, or banner will enhance the presentation. The purpose might be the lead-in for a presentation if it can be counted on to grab the interest of the listeners, in which case, the organization will be deductive. If it seems better to save the purpose until the end, the organization, of course, will be inductive.

The occasion, of course, plays an important role in the development and delivery of a presentation. A celebration speech when the company has achieved an important accomplishment will be organized around congratulating those who were most responsible for the accomplishment and giving some details about how it was achieved and probably something about the competition for the achievement. The presentation will be upbeat and not too long.

On the other hand, if bad news is being presented, it will probably be the CEO who is making the presentation and the bad-news announcement will come first followed with details about the news itself and how it came about, and probably end with a pep talk and encouragement to do better the next time.

Skill 3.2   Analyze the role of critical thinking skills in effective listening, speaking, and viewing.

Listening

Communication skills are crucial in a collaborative society. In particular, a person can not be a successful communicator without being an active listener. Focus on what others say, rather than planning on what to say next. By listening to everything another person is saying, you may pick up on natural cues that lead to the next conversation move without so much added effort.

Facilitating

It is quite acceptable to use standard opening lines to facilitate a conversation. Don't agonize over trying to come up with witty "one-liners," as the main obstacle in initiating conversation is just getting the first statement over with. After that, the real substance begins. A useful technique may be to make a comment or ask a question about a shared situation. This may be anything from the weather, to the food you are eating, to a new policy at work. Use an opener you are comfortable with, because most likely, your partner in conversation will be comfortable with it as well.

Stimulating Higher Level Critical Thinking Through Inquiry

Many people rely on questions to communicate with others. However, most fall back on simple clarifying questions rather than open-ended inquiries. Try to ask open-ended, deeper-level questions, since those tend to have the greatest reward and lead to a greater understanding. In answering those questions, more complex connections are made and more significant realizations are achieved.

Skill 3.3   Recognizing the role of body language, gestures, and visual aids in communicating a point of view in various cultures.

Physicality in a classroom calls for the performer to embody the emotion of the words into the motion of the character. This can drastically alter the perception of the character's personality, dilemma or situation.

Take a look at the phrase, "No, I don't mind waiting." Said while leaning back in a chair with a casual wave of the hand, the speaker comes off as easy going and calm. On the other hand, if the speaker is tapping their foot and constantly checking their watch, the message is very different. Simple gestures, from the raise of an eyebrow to a jump in the air, indicate the speaker's state of mind, supplementing vocal tone and inflection.

Physical techniques can be especially helpful for students that have trouble getting into their character. For young people who naturally gravitate towards physical activity, getting into the physical quality of a character can lead to the emotional quality as well. Ask students to draw on their own experiences to determine what the most natural physical expression would be. Generally, boys are more physically active than girls. They are willing to fall down, hunch over, jump on top of desks and dramatically exaggerate their movements to enhance the performance (or often just to be comical).

Also see Skill 1.4.

COMPETENCY 4.0 UNDERSTAND LISTENING AND SPEAKING FOR SOCIAL INTERACTION IN A VARIETY OF FORMAL AND INFORMAL SITUATIONS

Skill 4.1 Demonstrate knowledge of effective listening and speaking in conversation.

The successful conversationalist is a person who keeps up with what's going on in the world both far and near and ponders the meanings of events and developments. That person also usually reads about the topics that are of the most interest to him, both in printed materials and online. In addition, the effective conversationalist has certain areas that are of particular interest that have been probed in some depth. An interest in human behavior is usually one of this person's most particular interests. Why do people behave as they do? Why do some succeed and some fail? This person will also be interested in and concerned about social issues, particularly in the immediate community but also on a wider scale and will have ideas for solving some of those problems.

With all of this, the most important thing a good conversationalist can do is to *listen*, not just wait until the other person quits speaking so he or she can take the floor again but actually listening to learn what the other person has to say and also to learn more about that other person. Following a gathering, the best thing a person can think about another is that a person was interested enough to listen to the other's ideas and opinions, and that is the person who will be remembered the longest and with the most regard.

It's acceptable to be passionate about one's convictions in polite conversation; it is not acceptable to be overbearing or unwilling to hear and consider another's point of view. It's important to keep one's emotions under control in these circumstances even if the other person does not.

Skill 4.2   Examine techniques of effective listening and speaking in small- and large-group situations.

"Political correctness" is a new concept tossed around frequently in the 21st century. It has always existed, of course. The successful speaker of the 19th century understood and was sensitive to audiences. However, that person was typically a man, of course, and the only audience that was important was a male audience, and more often than not, the only important audience was a white one.

Many things have changed in discourse since the 19th century just as the society the speaker lives in and addresses has changed, and the speaker who disregards the existing conventions for "political correctness" usually finds himself/herself in trouble. Rap music makes a point of ignoring those conventions, particularly with regard to gender, and is often the target of very hostile attacks.

On the other hand, rap performers often intend to be revolutionary and have developed their own audiences and have become outrageously wealthy by exploiting those newly-developed audiences based primarily on thumbing their noses at establishment conventions.

Even so, the successful speaker must understand and be sensitive to what is current in "political correctness." The "n word" is a case in point. There was a time when that term was thrown about at will by politicians and other public speakers, but no more. Nothing could spell the end of a politician's career more certainly than using that term in his campaign or public addresses.

These terms are called "pejorative"—A word or phrase that expresses contempt or disapproval. Such terms as *redneck*, *queer*, or *cripple* may only be considered pejorative if used by a non-member of the group they apply to. For example, the "n word," which became very inflammatory in the 1960s, is now being used sometimes by African-American artists to refer to themselves, especially in their music, with the intention of underscoring their protest of the establishment.

References to gender have became particularly sensitive in the 20th century as a result of the women's rights movement, and the speaker who disregards these sensitivities does so at his/her peril. The generic "he" is no longer acceptable, and this requires a strategy to deal with pronominal references without repetitive he/she, his/her, etc. Several ways to approach this: switch to a passive construction that does not require a subject; switch back and forth, using the male pronoun in one reference and the female pronoun in another one, being sure to sprinkle them reasonably evenly; or switch to the plural. The last alternative is the one most often chosen. This requires some care, and the speaker should spend time developing these skills before stepping in front of an audience.

Debates and panel discussions fall under the umbrella of formal speaking, and the rules for formal speaking should apply here although lapsing into conversation language is acceptable. Swear words should be avoided in these situations.

A debate presents two sides of a debatable thesis—pro and con. Each side will posit a hypothesis, prove it, and defend it. A formal debate is a sort of formal dance with each side following a strictly defined format. However, within those guidelines, debaters are free to develop their arguments and rebuttals as they choose. The successful debater prepares by developing very thoroughly both sides of the thesis: "Mexico's border with the United States must be closed" and "Mexico's border with the United States must remain open." Debaters must be thoroughly prepared to argue their own side, but they must also have a strategy for rebutting the opposing side's arguments. All aspects of critical thinking and logical argument are employed, and the successful debaters will use ethical appeal (their own credibility) and emotional appeal to persuade the judges who will determine who wins—that is, the side that best establishes its thesis, proves it logically, but also *persuades* the audience to come over to its position.

A panel is typically composed of *experts* who explain and defend a particular topic. Often, panels will include representatives from more than one field of study and more than one position on the topic. Typically, each will have a limited amount of time to make an opening statement either presenting explanatory material or arguing a point of view. Then the meeting will be opened up to the audience for questions. A moderator will keep order and will control the time limits on the opening statements and responses and will sometimes intervene and ask a panel member that was not the target of a particular question from the audience to elaborate or rebut the answer of the panel member who was questioned. Panel are usually limited to four or five people although in special cases, they may be much larger.

Skill 4.3   Analyze factors affecting listening and speaking in various social contexts.

See Skill 3.1.

TEACHER CERTIFICATION STUDY GUIDE

DOMAIN II.   WRITING

COMPETENCY 5.0 UNDERSTAND WRITING FOR INFORMATION AND UNDERSTANDING

Skill 5.1   Evaluate information from various sources for use in a research project.

The best place to start research is usually at your local library. Not only does it have numerous books, videos, and periodicals to use for references, the librarian is always a valuable resource for information, or where to get that information.

"Those who declared librarians obsolete when the internet rage first appeared are now red-faced. We need them more than ever. The internet is full of 'stuff' but its value and readability is often questionable. 'Stuff' doesn't give you a competitive edge, high-quality related information does."
-Patricia Schroeder, President of the Association of American Publishers

The internet is a multi-faceted goldmine of information, but you must be careful to discriminate between reliable and unreliable sources. Stick to sites that are associated with an academic institution, whether it be a college or university or a scholarly organization.

Keep **content** and **context** in mind when researching. Don't be so wrapped up how you are going to apply your resource to your project that you miss the author's entire purpose or message. Remember that there are multiple ways to get the information you need. Read an encyclopedia article about your topic to get a general overview, and then focus in from there. Note important names of people associated with your subject, time periods, and geographic areas. Make a list of key words and their synonyms to use while searching for information. And finally, don't forget about articles in magazines and newspapers, or even personal interviews with experts related to your field of interest!

Skill 5.2   Revise drafts to improve their effectiveness.

When assessing and responding to student writing, there are several guidelines to remember.

Responding to non-graded writing (formative).

1. Avoid using a red pen. Whenever possible use a #2 pencil.
2. Explain the criteria that will be used for assessment in advance.
3. Read the writing once while asking the question, "Is the student's response appropriate for the assignment?"
4. Reread and make note at the end whether the student met the objective of the writing task.
5. Responses should be noncritical and use supportive and encouraging language.

MIDDLE LEVEL ENGLISH

6. Resist writing on or over the student's writing.
7. Highlight the ideas you wish to emphasize, question, or verify.
8. Encourage your students to take risks.

Responding to and evaluating graded writing (summative).

1. Ask students to submit prewriting and rough-draft materials including all revisions with their final draft.
2. For the first reading, use a holistic method, examining the work as a whole.
3. When reading the draft for the second time, assess it using the standards previously established.
4. Responses to the writing should be written in the margin and should use supportive language.
5. Make sure you address the process as well as the product. It is important that students value the learning process as well as the final product.
6. After scanning the piece a third time, write final comments at the end of the draft.

The most recent research reinforces what teachers have always known—that cooperative learning is a powerful strategy in the classroom. Cooperative or collaborative learning is working together as we have always tried to do, but with a new understanding about how groups work together, borrowed from the areas of communication and psychology. Grouping can be a very effective way to work, but it can also be very ineffective. So, the question becomes how can I maximize the productivity of groups? While you are experimenting, keep the following ideas in mind:

1. Cooperative learning allows teachers to move away from the center of the room and rely less on lecturing.

2. Cooperative learning gives students the opportunity to verbalize their ideas.

3. Cooperative learning gives students more ownership of what they learn and therefore motivates them more.

Listed below are the group skills that you will want to emphasize when working it groups. Also, you will find three strategies that work. It is important to provide peer-evaluation guidelines.

Guidelines for the writer

- Make a list of questions or concerns for your peers.

- Maintain an open attitude. It is important to use the evaluator's comments rather than being defensive. Keep in mind that the readers are only trying to help you.

Guidelines for the peer-evaluator

- Begin by pointing out the strengths first. Then, identify the areas that need to be improved.

- Provide encouragement and suggest things the writer can do to improve the piece of writing.

- Focus on content and organization. Avoid commenting on errors of punctuation or mechanics. These problems can be fixed during the editing stage.

- Be sensitive to the writer's feelings and give the peer-response your best effort.

When creating peer-response groups, keep in mind the following ideas.

1. Make sure each group is balanced with students of varying ability. Peer-response groups will not work effectively if all the strong writers are in one or two groups. Spread out the talents of the class evenly among the groups. It is usually better for the teacher to assign the groups because this method not only prevents hurt feelings, it also allows the teacher to balance the groups with varying academic abilities and skill levels to ensure maximum benefit for all students.

2. Allow the groups to work together for more than one session. It takes time to create a group that will work effectively together and for peers to become comfortable working together.

3. Don't expect groups to produce significant results initially. Remember evaluating and revising are the most demanding stages of writing.

When responding to student writing, there are a variety of approaches you can use depending on the focus and purpose of the assignment. You may want to vary the approaches.

- Analytical Evaluation identifies the qualities of a successful piece of writing and attributes point values for each aspect. The student's grade is determined by the point total. Students often like this type of evaluation since it is concrete and highlights specific strengths and weaknesses. One drawback for this type of evaluation is that it places a greater emphasis on the part rather than the whole.

- Holistic Scoring assesses a piece of writing as a whole. Usually a paper is read quickly through once to get a general impression. The writing is graded according to the impression of the whole work rather than the sum of its parts. Often holistic scoring uses a rubric that establishes the overall criteria for a certain score to evaluate each paper.

- A Performance System identifies established criteria, and as long as the student meets the acceptable level of activity, the points are awarded. This particular approach is useful for activities like journal writing.

- Portfolio Grading allows the students to select the pieces of work to be graded. Often this technique is used with writing workshops. Students often like this method because they have control over the evaluation process. Also, since teachers do not have to grade everything, it lessens their workload.

When the time comes to assign grades, keep a few things in mind.

1. Each piece of writing should have clearly established criteria.

2. Involve students in the process of defining the criteria. Students are more apt to understand criteria they have helped develop.

3. Give students numerous experiences with formative evaluation (evaluation as the student is writing the piece). Give students points for the work they have done throughout the process.

4. During the summative evaluation phase (final evaluation), students play an active role. Provide them with a form to identify the best parts of the writing and the things they would work on given more time.

5. Focus on content, fluency and freshness of ideas with young writers. Correctness and punctuation will follow as they gain control of the language.

Skill 5.3   **Apply skills for presenting and organizing content in informational writing.**

Organizational Structures

Authors use a particular organization to best present the concepts which they are writing about. Teaching students to recognize organizational structures helps them to understand authors' literary intentions, and helps them in deciding which structure to use in their own writing.

Cause and Effect: When writing about *why* things happen, as well as *what* happens, authors commonly use the cause and effect structure. For example, when writing about how he became so successful, a CEO might talk about how he excelled in math in high school, moved to New York after college, and stuck to his goals even after multiple failures. These are all *causes* that lead to the *effect*, or result, of him becoming a wealthy and powerful businessman.

Compare and Contrast: When examining the merits of multiple concepts or products, compare and contrast lends itself easily to organization of ideas. For example, a person writing about foreign policy in different countries will put them against each other to point out differences and similarities, easily highlighting the concepts the author wishes to emphasize.

Problem and Solution: This structure is used in a lot of handbooks and manuals. Anything organized around procedure-oriented tasks, such as a computer repair manual, gravitates toward a problem and solution format, because it offers such clear, sequential text organization.

TEACHER CERTIFICATION STUDY GUIDE

COMPETENCY 6.0 UNDERSTAND WRITING FOR PERSONAL EXPRESSION AND SOCIAL INTERACTION

Skill 6.1 Demonstrate awareness of connotation and figurative meaning in selecting language for a given expressive purpose.

Before assigning any other written work, familiarize students with definitions, examples, and detailed explanations of the following:

- connotation/connote
- denotation/denote
- figurative language/figurative meaning
- literal language/literal meaning
- symbol/symbolism/symbolize
- metaphor/mixed metaphor
- simile
- analogy/false analogy
- oxymoron
- cliché

With students working individually and/or in groups, ask them to evaluate and analyze, in writing, the connotations (as to social setting, the speaker, etc.), literal meanings, and contrasts in groups of topically related expressions, such as the following:

- Dinner is served, madam.
- Hey, let's hit the feedbag!

- Sigmund is a zombie.
- Poor Sigmund works so hard and looks so tired.

- Cassandra is an eloquent speaker.
- Pollyanna has a silver tongue.

Assign individual homework requiring students to incorporate literal and figurative language in an essay or story about a person, event, activity, or idea. Explain the necessity of unified imagery in a written work, the perils of clichés and mixed metaphors, and the need to avoid overwriting (see also **Skill 6.3**). If students are having trouble generating figurative language, suggest that they consider the following as potential sources of metaphors, similes, analogies, etc.:

- work
- play
- food
- sleep
- time
- love

MIDDLE LEVEL ENGLISH

- animals
- plants
- learning

Teachers may also wish to assign students the task of presenting and explaining to the class an example of figurative language from a favorite poem, song, or prose excerpt.

Lastly, since all language appeals to at least one of the senses, encourage students to look to sight, smell, hearing, touch, and taste as apt starting points for creating vivid written language, whether figurative or literal.

Skill 6.2   Judge alternative introductory or concluding sentences for a personal essay on a given theme.

Introductory Sentences

In order to gain favorable reader interest and attention, an essay's introduction should quickly and clearly give readers key information about the essay's theme. If a writer is in doubt about what this information is, she/he can follow the guideline commonly used by journalists when introducing a subject: Answer the questions Who? What? Where? When? How? and Why? as they pertain to one's theme. For example, consider the following introductory sentences.

- High school and college are very different.
- I find that high school and college are very different.
- During my first semester at Oklahoma State, I discovered that high school and college are very different.
- During my first semester at Oklahoma State, I discovered that campus life is freer and academic standards are tougher than at high school.

The first sentence answers only the thematic "what" question; the second only the "what" and "who." The third sentence adds answers to the "when" and "where" questions but, unlike the fourth sentence, remains vague as to just *how* college differs from high school. Ask students to evaluate the above sentences or similar examples for clarity and comprehensiveness.

Using the journalists' guidelines mentioned above, have students practice writing introductory sentences and paragraphs about a variety of personal essay subjects. After they have done this, provide them with some sample sentences in need of revision. For example:

- High school and college are very different. I discovered this during my first semester at Oklahoma State. I discovered that Oklahoma State's social life and academic life are very different than at high school.
- Sarah and Jeanne are sisters. They are identical twins. Both of them are on the high school volleyball team.

Emphasize the need to make multiple short sentences like those above into longer sentences. Doing so will avoid choppy, repetitive writing. Have students do the same with their own sentences wherever necessary.

Offer the following examples as common pitfalls to avoid when introducing an essay topic. Avoid distracting opening statements such as:

- "After carefully considering for a long time which topic to choose, I selected…" The reader doesn't need to know how much care or time goes into choosing a topic.
- "I chose this topic because it interests me very much." Readers will assume that writers are interested in their chosen topics.
- "This topic was very difficult for me but I decided to write about…" By itself, such a statement can seem like a kind of special pleading. Generally it is preferable to introduce a topic factually; any difficulties (complexity, controversy, etc.) can be addressed at the end of the introduction and/or in the body of the essay.

A final note: An essay's introductory paragraph/s should provide both a comprehensive account of what the topic is and what the writer is going to say about it. If the body or conclusion of an essay introduces perspectives and/or thematic material not covered in the introduction, readers may become confused. Have students check their writings for this before handing them in.

Concluding Sentences

Successful conclusions/concluding sentences accomplish several things:

- They provide a clear and concise summary of the essay's topic.
- They provide a decisive summary of the writer's view/s on the topic.

Ask students to evaluate and discuss the following concluding sentences (or similar examples).

- *Romeo and Juliet* is a lousy play.
- Well, I guess that *Romeo and Juliet* is a pretty good play.
- *Romeo and Juliet* shows us the lengths to which some people will go to oppose true love. Shakespeare shows his readers how hate is stronger than love.
- I was saddened by the play's tragic ending but was also deeply inspired by the emotional power of Romeo and Juliet's commitment to each other.

The first example is merely a sweeping dismissal. The second is indecisive. The third example is better than the first two but relies on vague expressions e.g., "some people," and "true love"; its conclusion is also rather simplistic. The final sentence is more specific in vocabulary, context, and point of view.

Have students work individually, in pairs, or in groups (or in a combination of all three) to write conclusions based on class reading assignments. This work should emphasize that one can "start" an essay with a conclusion, then work "backward" from there by giving support—through reasoning, quotations, data, character analyses, personal experiences or current events—for it. Teachers should also emphasize that conclusions will need to be altered or abandoned if support for them is lacking or contradicted by other factual evidence, perspectives, etc.

Skill 6.3 Analyze problems relating to the effectiveness of narrative or descriptive materials and identify appropriate revisions.

Some people say that God is in the details; others say that the devil is in the details. Either way, the message is the same with regards to vivid, informative writing: details are the key. Before assigning other written work, ask students to evaluate and analyze sentences such as the following for clarity and comprehensiveness.

- While walking I saw an accident.
- While walking to the store I saw a car accident.
- While walking to the drugstore last night, I saw a bad three-car accident in front of the gas station.

Each of these sentences report on the same event but only the last one meets the informative standard—the "journalistic guidelines"—explained in **Skill 6.2**. This sentence provides information that answers the who, what, where, and when aspects of the writer's chosen subject. Review the significance of this with students, then assign homework/class work accordingly.

Students also need to be aware of the pitfalls of providing too much information, especially redundant, marginal or irrelevant information, as in the following examples or ones like them. Have students point out, in writing, whatever is wrong with each example. Then have them revise each one.

- Last night 30 cm of cold white snow fell from the clouds in the sky above us.
- Before you swallow your food down into your stomach, you should chew it with your teeth.
- The great novelist hand-wrote his masterpiece novel on paper.

Students must also be made aware of how to "manage topic and time" in their writings. For example, in a 400-word essay assignment a topic such as "my year as a foreign exchange student in Germany" cannot likely be done justice: the timeframe is too long and the topic too broad for 400 words. Instead, encourage students to focus on smaller, more manageable topics. For example: "one big difference between German and American life," "a memorable day in my German neighborhood," etc. Less can be more. Emphasize this prior to assigning any written work.

Encourage students to write about what they know: the people in their lives, their personal experiences, opinions, their hobbies and interests, favorite literary works or music, sports, the future, etc. Assign written work accordingly.

Students who show an aptitude or interest for longer, even book-length, writing should be encouraged to take on larger topics and timeframes, perhaps as extra credit assignments.

Emphasize to students the importance of avoiding certain words and expressions that can either overstate a case, or leave no room for exceptions to it. Avoid readily falsifiable statements such as:

- "No-one thinks the way you do."
- "That's the way it's always been."
- "Everyone has always loved this song."

Have students revise all of the above into readily defensible statements. Teachers may also wish to provide students with a list of words to be especially careful with, lest a statement become an overstatement:

- always, never, forever, every time, any time
- no-one, nobody, none, all, every, everyone, everybody
- anywhere, everywhere, nowhere
- without exception, without a doubt

Skill 6.4   Apply strategies for composing personal texts.

When writing personal notes or letters, the writer needs to keep the following key matters in mind:

- Once the topic is determined, the writer must determine the appropriate tone to introduce and express it. Is humor appropriate? Seriousness? Bluntness or subtlety? Does the situation call for formal or informal language? The answers to these questions will depend, in good part, on the writer's relationship to the reader. Plan appropriately regarding situation and audience.
- Does the writer's introduction clearly explain the topic/situation to a reader who doesn't know or feel everything that the reader knows or feels? Don't assume that the writer and reader are "on the same page." Make a checklist to make sure that all key information is clearly and concisely expressed.
- If a note or letter involves a request, what type of response/result does the writer desire? Devise a strategy or strategies for achieving a desired outcome.
- If a note or letter involves a complaint about the reader, the writer will need to decide whether to ask for particular amends or to let the reader decide what, if anything, to do.
- If no amends are requested, the writer may wish to suggest ideas that would help to avoid similar conflicts in the future. Asking the reader for his or her opinions is also a possibility.
- If a timely response to any note or letter is needed, the writer must mention this.

Give students in-class opportunities to write a variety of personal notes and letters, whether involving "real life" or hypothetical situations. Invitations, thank-you notes, complaints, requests for favors, or personal updates are a few of the options available. Have students experiment with a variety of tones and strategies on a particular piece of personal correspondence, e.g., write a complaint letter in a blunt tone, then write the same complaint in a humorous tone; compare and contrast the drafts. Structure in-class activities to allow for peer feedback.

A final note: Remind students that e-mail messages, even if intended for just one reader, may eventually reach a much wider audience. In recent years there have been numerous instances of writers finding themselves in embarrassing situations or legal troubles due to their personal e-mails being circulated on the internet. If a writer is addressing a sensitive, unpleasant or controversial matter, he or she should consult state laws to determine whether or not personal correspondence is protected by privacy laws. If the law does protect such correspondence from being circulated by the addressee, then the writer may wish to mention this in his or her message. Otherwise, clarity, concision, and civility in written works provide a writer all the protection that he or she will likely need.

COMPETENCY 7.0 UNDERSTAND WRITING FOR CRITICAL ANALYSIS, EVALUATION, AND PERSUASION

Skill 7.1 Analyze the organization of an editorial or argumentative essay on a given topic.

Logical Argument

A logical argument consists of three stages.

First of all, the propositions which are necessary for the argument to continue are stated. These are called the premises of the argument. They are the evidence or reasons for accepting the argument and its conclusions.

Premises (or assertions) are often indicated by phrases such as "because", "since", "obviously" and so on. (The phrase "obviously" is often viewed with suspicion, as it can be used to intimidate others into accepting suspicious premises. If something doesn't seem obvious to you, don't be afraid to question it. You can always say "Oh, yes, you're right, it is obvious" when you've heard the explanation.)

Next, the premises are used to derive further propositions by a process known as inference. In inference, one proposition is arrived at on the basis of one or more other propositions already accepted. There are various forms of valid inference.

The propositions arrived at by inference may then be used in further inference. Inference is often denoted by phrases such as "implies that" or "therefore".

Finally, we arrive at the conclusion of the argument -- the proposition which is affirmed on the basis of the premises and inference. Conclusions are often indicated by phrases such as "therefore", "it follows that", "we conclude" and so on. The conclusion is often stated as the final stage of inference.

Classical Argument

In its simplest form, the classical argument has five main parts:

The **introduction**, which warms up the audience, establishes goodwill and rapport with the readers, and announces the general theme or thesis of the argument.

The **narration**, which summarizes relevant background material, provides any information the audience needs to know about the environment and circumstances that produce the argument, and set up the stakes–what's at risk in this question.

The **confirmation**, which lays out in a logical order (usually strongest to weakest or most obvious to most subtle) the claims that support the thesis, providing evidence for each claim.

The **refutation and concession**, which looks at opposing viewpoints to the writer's claims, anticipating objections from the audience, and allowing as much of the opposing viewpoints as possible without weakening the thesis.

The **summation**, which provides a strong conclusion, amplifying the force of the argument, and showing the readers that this solution is the best at meeting the circumstances.

Skill 7.2 Distinguish reasons, examples, or details that support a given argument or opinion.

Once a thesis is put forth, there are various ways to support it. The most obvious one is reasons. Usually a reason will answer the question why. Another technique is to give examples. A third is to give details.

The presentation of a prosecutor in a court trial is a good example of an argument that uses all of these.

The **thesis** of the prosecutor may be: John O'Hara stole construction materials from a house being built at 223 Hudson Ave. by the Jones Construction Company. As a **reason**, he might cite the following: He is building his own home on Green Street and needs materials and tools. This will answer the question why. He might give **examples**: 20 bags of concrete disappeared the night before Mr. O'Hara poured the basement for his house on Green Street. The electronic nail-setter disappeared from the building site on Hudson Ave. the day before Mr. O'Hara began to erect the frame of his house on Green Street. He might fill in the **details**: Mr. O'Hara's truck was observed by a witness on Hudson Ave. in the vicinity of the Jones Construction Company site the night the concrete disappeared. Mr. O'Hara's truck was observed again on that street by a witness the night the nail-setter disappeared.

Another example of a trial might be: **Thesis**, Adam Andrews murdered Joan Rogers in cold blood on the night of December 20. **Reason #1**: She was about to reveal their affair to his wife. **Reason #2**: Andrews' wife would inherit half of his sizeable estate in case of a divorce since there is no prenuptial agreement. **Example #1**: Rogers has demonstrated that he is capable of violence in an incident with a partner in his firm. **Example #2**: Rogers has had previous affairs where he was accused of violence. **Detail #1**: Andrews' wife once called the police and signed a warrant. **Detail #2**: A previous lover sought police protection from Andrews.

An **opinion** is a thesis and requires support. It can also use reasons, examples, and details.

For example:

Opinion: Our borders must be protected.

Reason #1: Terrorists can get into the country undetected. **Example #1**: An Iranian national was able to cross the Mexican border and live in this country for years before being detected. **Detail**: The Iranian national came up through Central America to Mexico then followed the route that Mexican illegal immigrants regularly took. **Example #2**: a group of Middle Eastern terrorists were arrested in Oregon after they had crossed the Canadian border. **Detail**: There was no screening at that border.

Reason #2: Illegal aliens are an enormous drain on resources such as health care. **Example**: The states of California and Texas bear enormous burdens for health care and education for illegal immigrants. **Detail**: Legal citizens are often denied care in those states because resources are stretched so thin.

Skill 7.3   Apply strategies for developing and evaluating persuasive writing.

Analyzing your Audience

- **Values**- What is important to this group of people? What is their background and how will that affect their perception of your speech?
- **Needs**- Find out in advance what the audience's needs are. Why are they listening to you? Find a way to satisfy their needs.
- **Constraints**- What might hold the audience back from being fully engaged in what you are saying, or agreeing with your point of view, or processing what you are trying to say? These could be political reasons, which make them wary of your presentation's ideology from the start, or knowledge reasons, in which the audience lacks the appropriate background information to grasp your ideas. Avoid this last constraint by staying away from technical terminology, slang, or abbreviations that may be unclear to your audience.
- **Demographic Information**- Take the audience's size into account, as well as the location of the presentation.

Start where the listeners are, and then take them where you want to go!

It's not necessary to write "I believe that . . . ." for a statement to be attributed to the writer. The very fact that it comes from him or her assumes that. The judgment should be stated simply and positively rather than negatively. If the statement has multiple phrases and clauses, developing it will be complicated. A simple, straightforward statement is better. For example: "The Mexican border should be closed." If another clause is added: "The Mexican border should be closed and all illegal immigrants should be sent home," then both issues must be proven and substantiated, and the reasoning tends to become confusing and muddy.

Once a position is taken, then reasons must be formulated: Terrorists can come across the open border; finding solutions to the increasing numbers of illegal immigrants becomes more difficult every year; it will be possible to control immigration with a closed border. Each of those points can be developed with reasoning and examples.

To avoid bias, all points of view must be taken into account. A good exercise is to argue the opposing point of view in order to understand the opposition. Also, establishing one's own credibility in a paper where there will be a strong counter-argument is helpful. The writer can demonstrate why he/she has no personal interest in either side, which will focus the writing on the reasoning rather than on the writer.

COMPETENCY 8.0 UNDERSTAND HOW TO USE THE WRITING PROCESS TO DEVELOP AND REFINE WRITTEN TEXTS

Skill 8.1 Apply strategies for generating ideas before writing.

Prior to writing, you will need to prewrite for ideas and details as well as decide how the essay will be organized. In the hour you have to write you should spend no more than 5-10 minutes prewriting and organizing your ideas. As you prewrite, it might be helpful to remember you should have at least three main points and at least two to three details to support your main ideas. There are several types of graphic organizers that you should practice using as you prepare for the essay portion of the test.

PRACTICE - Choose a topic complete the cluster.

PREWRITE TO EXPLAIN HOW OR WHY

Reread a question from the chart on the previous page that asks you to explain how a poet creates tone and mood use imagery and word choice. Then fill out the organizer on the following page that identifies how the poet effectively creates tone and mood. Support with examples from the poem.

VISUAL ORGANIZER: GIVING REASONS

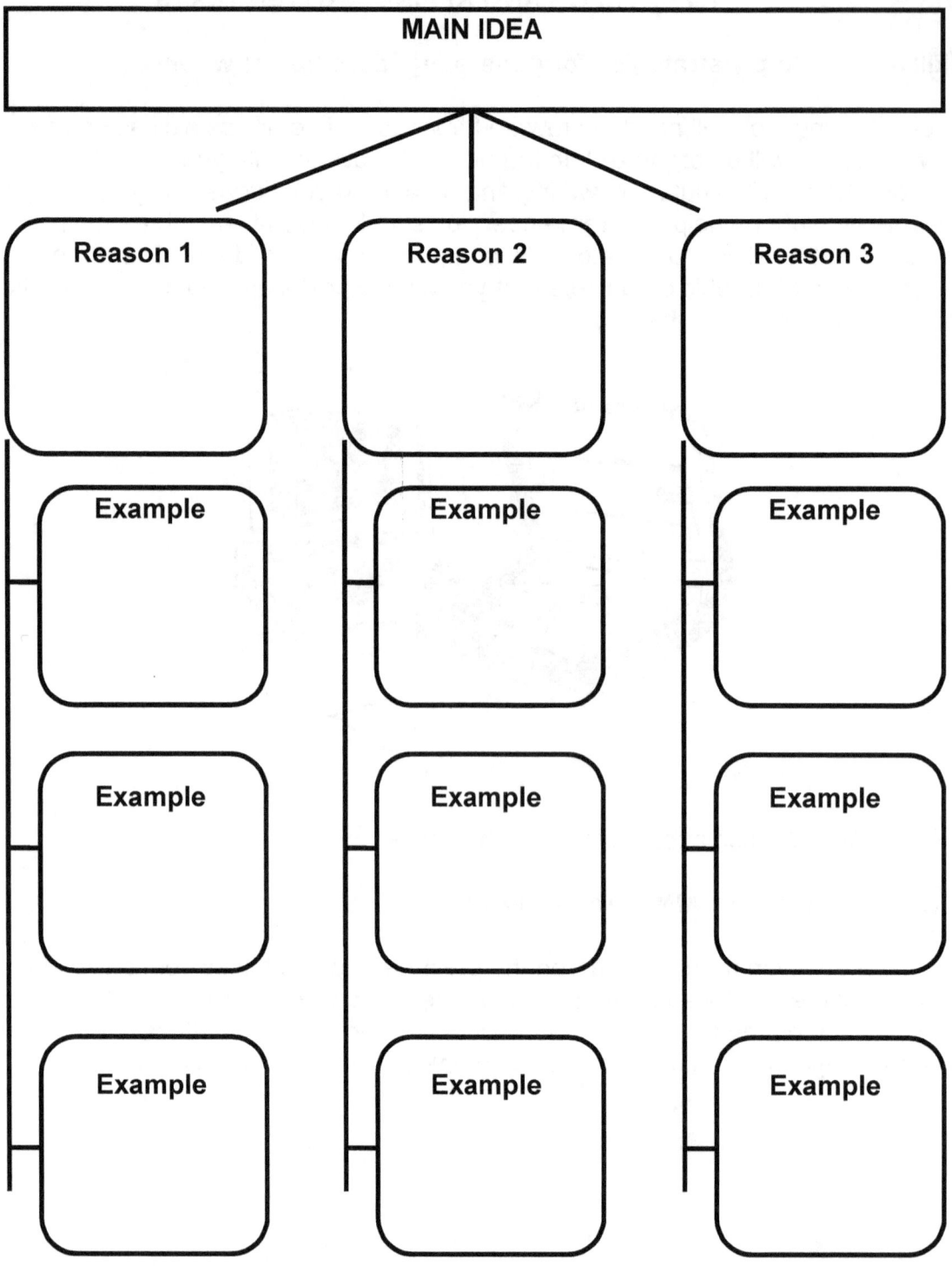

STEP 3: PREWRITE TO ORGANIZE IDEAS

After you have completed a graphic organizer, you need to decide how you will organize your essay. To organize your essay, you might consider one of the following patterns to structure your essay.

1. Examine individual elements such as **plot**, **setting**, **theme**, **character**, **point of view**, **tone**, **mood**, or **style**.

   SINGLE ELEMENT OUTLINE
   Intro - main idea statement
   Main point 1 with at least two supporting details
   Main point 2 with at least two supporting details
   Main point 3 with at least two supporting details
   Conclusion (restates main ideas and summary of main pts)

2. **Compare and contrast two elements**.

POINT-BY-POINT	BLOCK
Introduction Statement of main idea about A and B	Introduction Statement of main idea about A and B
Main Point 1 Discussion of A Discussion of B	Discussion of A Main Point 1 Main Point 2 Main point 3
Main Point 2 Discussion of A Discussion of B	Discussion of B Main Point 1 Main Point 2 Main Point 3
Main Point 3 Discussion of A Discussion of B	Conclusion Restate main idea
Conclusion Restatement or summary of main idea	

PRACTICE:
Using the cluster on the next page, choose an organizing chart and complete for your topic.

MIDDLE LEVEL ENGLISH

VISUAL ORGANIZER: GIVING INFORMATION

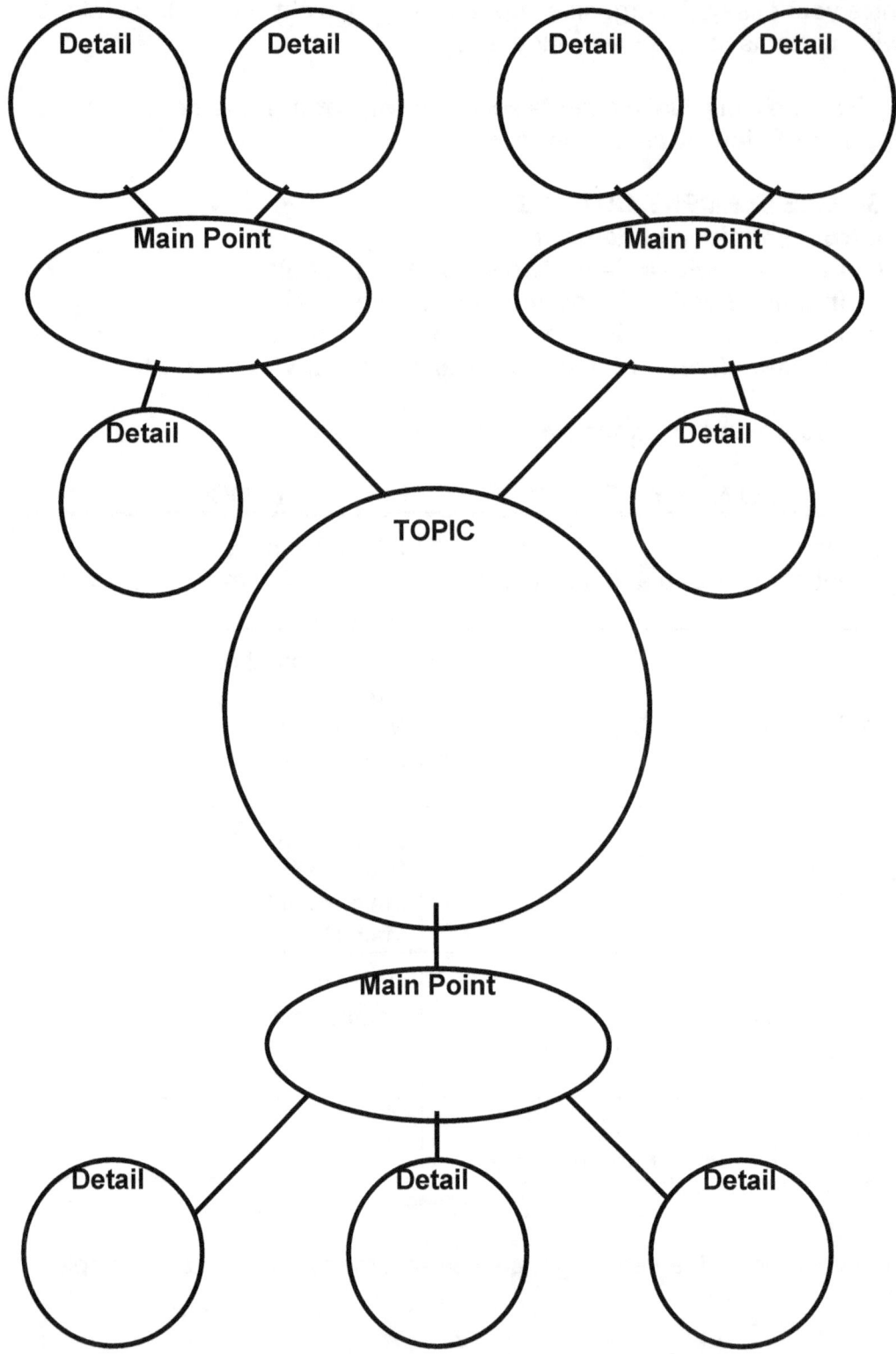

Skill 8.2   Demonstrate knowledge of procedures for drafting written texts.

Seeing writing as a process is very helpful in saving preparation time, particularly in the taking of notes and the development of drafts. Once a decision is made about the topic to be developed, some preliminary review of literature is helpful in thinking about the next step, which is to determine what the purpose of the written document will be. For example, if the topic is immigration, a cursory review of the various points of view in the debate going on in the country will help the writer decide what this particular written piece will try to accomplish. The purpose could just be a review of the various points of view, which would be an informative purpose. On the other hand, the writer might want to take a point of view and provide proof and support with the purpose of changing the reader's mind. The writer might even want the reader to take some action as the result of reading. Another possible purpose might be simply to write a description of a family of immigrants.

Once that cursory review has been completed, it's time to begin research in earnest and to prepare to take notes. If the thesis has been clearly defined, and some thought has been given to what will be used to prove or support it, a tentative outline can be developed. A thesis plus three points is typical. Decisions about introduction and conclusion should be deferred until the body of the paper is written. Note-taking is much more effective if the notes are being taken to provide information for an outline. There is much less danger that the writer will go off on time-consuming tangents.

Formal outlines inhibit effective writing. However, a loosely constructed outline can be an effective device for note-taking that will yield the information for a worthwhile statement about a topic. Sentence outlines are better than topic outlines because they require the writer to do some thinking about the direction a subtopic will take.

Once this preliminary note-taking phase is over, the first draft can be developed. The writing at this stage is likely to be highly individualistic. However, successful writers tend to just write, keeping in mind the purpose of the paper, the point that is going to be made in it, and the information that has been turned up in the research. Student writers need to understand that this first draft is just that—the first one. It takes more than one draft to write a worthwhile statement about a topic. This is what successful writers do. It's sometimes helpful to have students read the various drafts of a story by a well-known writer.

Once the draft is on paper, a stage that is sometimes called editing occurs. With word processors, this is much more easily achieved than in the past. Sections can be deleted, words can be changed, and additions can be made without doing the entire project over a second time.

What to look for: mechanics, of course, spelling, punctuation, etc., but it's important that student writers not mistake that for editing.

Editing is rereading objectively, testing the effectiveness on a reader of the arrangement and the line of reasoning. The kinds of changes that will need to be made are: rearranging the parts, adding information that is missing and needed, and deleting information that doesn't fit or contribute to the accomplishment of the purpose.

Once the body of the paper has been shaped to the writer's satisfaction, the introduction and conclusion should be fashioned. An introduction should grab the reader's interest and, perhaps, announce the purpose and thesis of the paper unless the reasoning is inductive, in which case, purpose and thesis may come later in the paper. The conclusion is to reaffirm the purpose in some way.

Skill 8.3   Apply strategies for revising and editing written materials.

Sometimes this exercise is seen by students as simply catching errors in spelling or word use. Students need to reframe their thinking about revising and editing. Some questions that need to be asked:

- Is the reasoning coherent?
- Is the point established?
- Does the introduction make the reader want to read this discourse?
- What is the thesis? Is it proven?
- What is the purpose? Is it clear? Is it useful, valuable, interesting?
- Is the style of writing so wordy that it exhausts the reader and interferes with engagement?
- Is the writing so spare that it is boring?
- Are the sentences too uniform in structure?
- Are there too many simple sentences?
- Are too many of the complex sentences the same structure?
- Are the compounds truly compounds or are they unbalanced?
- Are parallel structures truly parallel?
- If there are characters, are they believable?
- If there is dialogue, is it natural or stilted?
- Is the title appropriate?
- Does the writing show creativity or is it boring?
- Is the language appropriate? Is it too formal? Too informal? If jargon is used, is it appropriate?

Studies have clearly demonstrated that the most fertile area in teaching writing is this one. If students can learn to revise their own work effectively, they are well on their way to becoming effective, mature writers. Word processing is an important tool for teaching this stage in the writing process. Microsoft Word has tracking features that make the revision exchanges between teachers and students more effective than ever before.

COMPETENCY 9.0 EDIT WRITTEN TEXTS TO ACHIEVE CLARITY, UNITY, AND EFFECTIVE ORGANIZATION

Skill 9.1 Revising sentences to eliminate wordiness, ambiguity, and redundancy.

Enhancing Interest:

- Start out with an attention-grabbing introduction. This sets an engaging tone for the entire piece and will be more likely to pull the reader in.
- Use dynamic vocabulary and varied sentence beginnings. Keep the reader on their toes. If they can predict what you are going to say next, switch it up.
- Avoid using clichés (as cold as ice, the best thing since sliced bread, nip it in the bud). These are easy shortcuts, but they are not interesting, memorable, or convincing.

Ensuring Understanding:

- Avoid using the words, "clearly," "obviously," and "undoubtedly." Often, things that are clear or obvious to the author are not as apparent to the reader. Instead of using these words, make your point so strongly that it is clear on its own.
- Use the word that best fits the meaning you intend for, even if they are longer or a little less common. Try to find a balance, a go with a familiar yet precise word.
- When in doubt, explain further.

Techniques to Maintain Focus:

- **Focus on a main point.** The point should be clear to readers, and all sentences in the paragraph should relate to it.
- **Start the paragraph with a topic sentence.** This should be a general, one-sentence summary of the paragraph's main point, relating both back towards the thesis and toward the content of the paragraph. (A topic sentence is sometimes unnecessary if the paragraph continues a developing idea clearly introduced in a preceding paragraph, or if the paragraph appears in a narrative of events where generalizations might interrupt the flow of the story.)
- **Stick to the point.** Eliminate sentences that do not support the topic sentence.

Be flexible. If there is not enough evidence to support the claim your topic sentence is making, do not fall into the trap of wandering or introducing new ideas within the paragraph. Either find more evidence, or adjust the topic sentence to collaborate with the evidence that is available.

Redundancy

Incorrect: Joyce made sure that when her plane arrived that she retrieved all of her luggage.
Correct: Joyce made sure that when her plane arrived she retrieved all of her luggage.

Incorrect: He was a mere skeleton of his former self.
Correct: He was a skeleton of his former self.

Skill 9.2 Revise sentences and passages to subordinate ideas, maintain parallel form, and connect related ideas.

Students need to be trained to become effective at proofreading, revising and editing strategies. Begin by training them using both desk-side and scheduled conferences. Listed below are some strategies to use to guide students through the final stages of the writing process.

* Provide some guide sheets or forms for students to use during peer responses.

* Allow students to work in pairs and limit the agenda.

* Model the use of the guide sheet or form for the entire class.

* Give students a time limit.

  - Have the students read their partners' papers and ask at least three who, what, when, why, how questions. The students answer the questions and use them as a place to begin discussing the piece.

Provide students with a series of questions that will assist them in revising their writing.

1. Do the details give a clear picture? Add details that appeal to more than just the sense of sight.

2. How effectively are the details organized? Reorder the details if it is needed.

3. Are the thoughts and feelings of the writer included? Add personal thoughts and feelings about the subject.

As you discuss revision, you begin with discussing the definition of revise. Also, state that all writing must be revised to improve it. After students have revised their writing, it is time for the final editing and proofreading. There are a few key points to remember when helping students learn to edit and proofread their work.

* It is crucial that students are not taught grammar in isolation, but in context of the writing process.

* At this point in the writing process a mini-lesson that focuses on some of the problems your students are having would be appropriate.

* Ask students to read their writing and check for specific errors like using a subordinate clause as a sentence.

* Provide students with a proofreading checklist to guide them as they edit their work.

Skill 9.3 Solve problems related to text organization.

In studies of professional writers and how they produce their successful works, it has been revealed that writing is a process that can be clearly defined although in practice it must have enough flexibility to allow for creativity. The teacher must be able to define the various stages that a successful writer goes through in order to make a statement that has value. There must be a discovery stage when ideas, materials, supporting details, etc., are deliberately collected. These may come from many possible sources: the writer's own experience and observations, deliberate research of written sources, interviews of live persons, television presentations, or the internet.

The next stage is organization where the purpose, thesis, and supporting points are determined. Most writers will put forth more than one possible thesis and in the next stage, the writing of the paper, settle on one as the result of trial and error. Once the paper is written, the editing stage is necessary and is probably the most important stage. This is not just the polishing stage. At this point, decisions must be made regarding whether the reasoning is cohesive—does it hold together? Is the arrangement the best possible one or should the points be rearranged? Are there holes that need to be filled in? What form will the introduction take? Does the conclusion lead the reader out of the discourse or is it inadequate or too abrupt, etc.

It's important to remember that the best writers engage in all of these stages recursively. They may go back to discovery at any point in the process. They may go back and rethink the organization, etc. To help students become effective writers, the teacher needs to give them adequate practice in the various stages and encourage them to engage deliberately in the creative thinking that makes writers successful.

Skill 9.4 Use descriptive language and varied sentence structure to enhance writing.

See Skill 9.1.

COMPETENCY 10.0 APPLY KNOWLEDGE OF STANDARD ENGLISH GRAMMAR, USAGE, AND MECHANICS

Skill 10.1 Revise syntactic errors in a text.

Types of Clauses

Clauses are connected word groups that are composed of *at least* one subject and one verb. (A subject is the doer of an action or the element that is being joined. A verb conveys either the action or the link.)

Students are waiting for the start of the assembly.
Subject   Verb

At the end of the play, students wait for the curtain to come down.
               Subject Verb

Clauses can be independent or dependent.

Independent clauses can stand alone or can be joined to other clauses.

Independent clause	for and nor	
Independent clause,	but or yet so	Independent clause
Independent clause	;	Independent clause
Dependent clause	,	Independent clause
Independent clause		Dependent clause

Dependent clauses, by definition, contain at least one subject and one verb. However, they cannot stand alone as a complete sentence. They are structurally dependent on the main clause.

There are two types of dependent clauses: (1) those with a subordinating conjunction, and (2) those with a relative pronoun

Sample coordinating conjunctions:
Although
When
If
Unless
Because

Unless a cure is discovered, many more people will die of the disease.
    Dependent clause   +   Independent clause

Sample relative pronouns:
Who
Whom
Which
That

The White House has an official website, which contains press releases, news updates, and biographies of the President and Vice-President.
(Independent clause + relative pronoun + relative dependent clause)

Skill 10.2   Revise misplaced or dangling modifiers.

Particular phrases that are not placed near the one word they modify often result in misplaced modifiers. Particular phrases that do not relate to the subject being modified result in dangling modifiers.

Error: Weighing the options carefully, a decision was made regarding the punishment of the convicted murderer.

Problem: Who is weighing the options? No one capable of weighing is named in the sentence; thus, the participle phrase weighing the options carefully dangles. This problem can be corrected by adding a subject of the sentence capable of doing the action.

Correction: Weighing the options carefully, the judge made a decision regarding the punishment of the convicted murderer.

Error: Returning to my favorite watering hole, brought back many fond memories.

Problem: The person who returned is never indicated, and the participle phrase dangles. This problem can be corrected by creating a dependent clause from the modifying phrase.

Correction: When I returned to my favorite watering hole, many fond memories came back to me.

Error: One damaged house stood only to remind townspeople of the hurricane.

Problem: The placement of the misplaced modifier only suggests that the sole reason the house remained was to serve as a reminder. The faulty modifier creates ambiguity.

Correction: Only one damaged house stood, reminding townspeople of the hurricane.

Skill 10.3   **Revise nonstandard capitalization, punctuation, and spelling.**

Spelling

Concentration in this section will be on spelling plurals and possessives. The multiplicity and complexity of spelling rules based on phonics, letter doubling, and exceptions to rules - not mastered by adulthood - should be replaced by a good dictionary. As spelling mastery is also difficult for adolescents, our recommendation is the same. Learning the use of a dictionary and thesaurus will be a more rewarding use of time.

Most plurals of nouns that end in hard consonants or hard consonant sounds followed by a silent *e* are made by adding *s*. Some words ending in vowels only add *s*.

    fingers, numerals, banks, bugs, riots, homes, gates, radios, bananas

Nouns that end in soft consonant sounds *s, j, x, z, ch,* and *sh*, add *es*. Some nouns ending in *o* add es.

    dresses, waxes, churches, brushes, tomatoes, potatoes

Nouns ending in *y* preceded by a vowel just add *s*.

    boys, alleys

Nouns ending in *y* preceded by a consonant change the *y* to *i* and add *es*.

    babies, corollaries, frugalities, poppies

Some nouns plurals are formed irregularly or remain the same.

    sheep, deer, children, leaves, oxen

Some nouns derived from foreign words, especially Latin, may make their plurals in two different ways - one of them Anglicized. Sometimes, the meanings are the same; other times, the two plurals are used in slightly different contexts. It is always wise to consult the dictionary.

    appendices, appendixes   criterion, criteria
    indexes, indices   crisis, crises

Make the plurals of closed (solid) compound words in the usual way except for words ending in *ful* which make their plurals on the root word.

    timelines, hairpins, cupsful

Make the plurals of open or hyphenated compounds by adding the change in inflection to the word that changes in number.

>fathers-in-law, courts-martial, masters of art, doctors of medicine

Make the plurals of letters, numbers, and abbreviations by adding *s*.

fives and tens, IBMs, 1990s, *p*s and *q*s (Note that letters are italicized.)

Capitalization

Capitalize all proper names of persons (including specific organizations or agencies of government); places (countries, states, cities, parks, and specific geographical areas); and things (political parties, structures, historical and cultural terms, and calendar and time designations); and religious terms (any deity, revered person or group, sacred writings).

>Percy Bysshe Shelley, Argentina, Mount Rainier National Park, Grand Canyon, League of Nations, the Sears Tower, Birmingham, Lyric Theater, Americans, Midwesterners, Democrats, Renaissance, Boy Scouts of America, Easter, God, Bible, Dead Sea Scrolls, Koran

Capitalize proper adjectives and titles used with proper names.

California gold rush, President John Adams, French fries, Homeric epic, Romanesque architecture, Senator John Glenn

Note: Some words that represent titles and offices are not capitalized unless used with a proper name.

Capitalized	Not Capitalized
Congressman McKay	the congressman from Florida
Commander Alger	commander of the Pacific Fleet
Queen Elizabeth	the queen of England

Capitalize all main words in titles of works of literature, art, and music. (See "Using Italics" in the Punctuation section.)

The candidate should be cognizant of proper rules and conventions of punctuation, capitalization, and spelling. Competency exams will generally test the ability to apply the more advanced skills; thus, a limited number of more frustrating rules is presented here. Rules should be applied according to the American style of English, i.e. spelling *theater* instead of *theatre* and placing terminal marks of punctuation almost exclusively within other marks of punctuation.

Punctuation

Using terminal punctuation in relation to quotation marks

In a quoted statement that is either declarative or imperative, place the period inside the closing quotation marks.

"The airplane crashed on the runway during takeoff."

If the quotation is followed by other words in the sentence, place a comma inside the closing quotations marks and a period at the end of the sentence.

"The airplane crashed on the runway during takeoff," said the announcer.

In most instances in which a quoted title or expression occurs at the end of a sentence, the period is placed before either the single or double quotation marks.

"The middle school readers were unprepared to understand Bryant's poem 'Thanatopsis.'"

Early book-length adventure stories like *Don Quixote* and *The Three Musketeers* were known as "picaresque novels."

There is an instance in which the final quotation mark would precede the period - if the content of the sentence were about a speech or quote so that the understanding of the meaning would be confused by the placement of the period.

The first thing out of his mouth was "Hi, I'm home."
but
The first line of his speech began "I arrived home to an empty house".

In sentences that are interrogatory or exclamatory, the question mark or exclamation point should be positioned outside the closing quotation marks if the quote itself is a statement or command or cited title.

Who decided to lead us in the recitation of the "Pledge of Allegiance"?

Why was Tillie shaking as she began her recitation, "Once upon a midnight dreary..."?

I was embarrassed when Mrs. White said, "Your slip is showing"!

In sentences that are declarative but the quotation is a question or an exclamation, place the question mark or exclamation point inside the quotation marks.

The hall monitor yelled, "Fire! Fire!"

MIDDLE LEVEL ENGLISH

"Fire! Fire!" yelled the hall monitor.

Cory shrieked, "Is there a mouse in the room?" (In this instance, the question supersedes the exclamation.)

Using periods with parentheses or brackets

Place the period inside the parentheses or brackets if they enclose a complete sentence, independent of the other sentences around it.

Stephen Crane was a confirmed alcohol and drug addict. (He admitted as much to other journalists in Cuba.)

If the parenthetical expression is a statement inserted within another statement, the period in the enclosure is omitted.

Mark Twain used the character Indian Joe (He also appeared in *The Adventures of Tom Sawyer*) as a foil for Jim in *The Adventures of Huckleberry Finn*.

When enclosed matter comes at the end of a sentence requiring quotation marks, place the period outside the parentheses or brackets.

"The secretary of state consulted with the ambassador [Albright]."

Using commas

Separate two or more coordinate adjectives, modifying the same word and three or more nouns, phrases, or clauses in a list.

Maggie's hair was dull, dirty, and lice-ridden.

Dickens portrayed the Artful Dodger as skillful pickpocket, loyal follower of Fagin, and defendant of Oliver Twist.

Ellen daydreamed about getting out of the rain, taking a shower, and eating a hot dinner.

In Elizabethan England, Ben Johnson wrote comedy, Christopher Marlowe wrote tragedies, and William Shakespeare composed both.

Use commas to separate antithetical or complimentary expressions from the rest of the sentence.

The veterinarian, not his assistant, would perform the delicate surgery.

The more he knew about her, the less he wished he had known.

Randy hopes to, and probably will, get an appointment to the Naval Academy.

His thorough, though esoteric, scientific research could not easily be understood by high school students.

Using double quotation marks with other punctuation

Quotations - whether words, phrases, or clauses - should be punctuated according to the rules of the grammatical function they serve in the sentence.

The works of Shakespeare, "the bard of Avon," have been contested as originating with other authors.

"You'll get my money," the old man warned, "when 'Hell freezes over'."

Sheila cited the passage that began "Four score and seven years ago...." (Note the ellipsis followed by an enclosed period.)

"Old Ironsides" inspired the preservation of the U.S.S. Constitution. Use quotation marks to enclose the titles of shorter works: songs, short poems, short stories, essays, and chapters of books. (See "Using Italics" for punctuating longer titles.)

"The Tell-Tale Heart"   "Casey at the Bat"   "America the Beautiful"

Using semicolons

Use semicolons to separate independent clauses when the second clause is introduced by a transitional adverb. (These clauses may also be written as separate sentences, preferably by placing the adverb within the second sentence.)

The Elizabethans modified the rhyme scheme of the sonnet; thus, it was called the English sonnet.
or
The Elizabethans modified the rhyme scheme of the sonnet. It thus was called the English sonnet.

Use semicolons to separate items in a series that are long and complex or have internal punctuation.

The Italian Renaissance produced masters in the fine arts: Dante Alighieri, author of the *Divine Comedy;* Leonardo da Vinci, painter of *The Last Supper;* and Donatello, sculptor of the *Quattro Coronati*, the four saints.

The leading scorers in the WNBA were Haizhaw Zheng, averaging 23.9 points per game; Lisa Leslie, 22; and Cynthia Cooper, 19.5.

Using colons

Place a colon at the beginning of a list of items. (Note its use in the sentence about Renaissance Italians on the previous page.)

> The teacher directed us to compare Faulkner's three symbolic novels: *Absalom, Absalom; As I Lay Dying;* and *Light in August.*

Do **not** use a comma if the list is preceded by a verb.

> Three of Faulkner's symbolic novels are *Absalom, Absalom; As I Lay Dying,* and *Light in August.*

Using dashes

Place dashes to denote sudden breaks in thought.

> Some periods in literature - the Romantic Age, for example - spanned different time periods in different countries.

Use dashes instead of commas if commas are already used elsewhere in the sentence for amplification or explanation.

> The Fireside Poets included three Brahmans - James Russell Lowell, Henry David Wadsworth, Oliver Wendell Holmes - and John Greenleaf Whittier.

Use italics to punctuate the titles of long works of literature, names of periodical publications, musical scores, works of art and motion picture television, and radio programs. (When unable to write in italics, students should be instructed to underline in their own writing where italics would be appropriate.)

> *The Idylls of the King* *Hiawatha* *The Sound and the Fury*
> *Mary Poppins* *Newsweek* *The Nutcracker Suite*

DOMAIN III. READING

COMPETENCY 11.0 APPLY SKILLS FOR READING FOR INFORMATION AND UNDERSTANDING

Skill 11.1 Identify and apply distinctions between general statements and specific details.

From general to specific is a continuum. In other words, a term or phrase may be more specific than another term or more general than another one. For example, car is about the middle of the continuum; however, if I mention John Smith's car, it has become more specific. The most specific is a unique item: John Smith's 2007 Lexus, serial #000000000. Cars is a general term that can be narrowed and narrowed and narrowed to suit whatever purposes the writer has for the term. For instance, it would be possible to make a statement about all the cars in the United States, which has been narrowed somewhat from cars. It is, however, a very general term. A thesis statement is typically a generality: All the cars in the United States run on gasoline. Then specifics would be needed to prove that generalization.

In developing a line of reasoning, the choice will be either inductive, going from the specific to the general, or deductive, going from the general to the specific. Inductive reasoning might be as follows: "I tasted a green apple from my grandfather's yard when I was five years old, and it was sour. I also tasted a green apple that my friend brought to school in his lunchbox when I was eight years old, and it was sour. I was in Browns' roadside market and bought some green Granny Smith apples last week, and they were sour." This is a series of specifics. From those specifics, I might draw a conclusion—a generalization—all apples are sour, and I would have reasoned inductively to arrive at that generalization.

The same simplistic argument developed deductively would begin with the generalization: all apples are sour. Then specifics would be offered to support that generalization: the sour green apple I tasted in my grandfather's orchard, the sour green apple in my friend's lunchbox, the Granny Smith apples from the market.

When reasoning is this simple and straightforward, it's easy to follow, but it's also easy to see fallacies. For example, this person hasn't tasted all the green apples in the world; and, in fact, some green apples are not sour. However, it's rarely that easy to see the generalizations and the specifics. In determining whether a point has been proven, it's necessary to do that.

Sometimes generalizations are cited on the assumption that they are commonly accepted and do not need to be supported. An example: all men die sooner or later. Examples wouldn't be needed because that is commonly accepted. Now, some people might require that "die" be defined, but even the definition of "die" is assumed in this generalization.

Some current generalizations that may assume common acceptance: Providing healthcare for all citizens is the responsibility of the government. All true patriots will support any war the government declares.

Flaws in argument, either intended or unintended, frequently have to do with generalizations and specifics. Are the specifics sufficient to prove the truth of the generality? Does a particular specific actually apply to this generalization? Many times it will depend on definitions. The question can always be asked: has the writer (or speaker) established the generalization?

Skill 11.2   Draw conclusions from a given passage or visual message.

A common fallacy in reasoning is the *post hoc ergo propter hoc* ("after this, therefore because of this") or the false-cause fallacy. These occur in cause/effect reasoning, which may either go from cause to effect or effect to cause. They happen when an inadequate cause is offered for a particular effect; when the possibility of more than one cause is ignored; and when a connection between a particular cause and a particular effect is not made.

An example of a *post hoc*: Our sales shot up thirty-five percent after we ran that television campaign; therefore the campaign caused the increase in sales. It might have been a cause, of course, but more evidence is needed to prove it.

An example of an inadequate cause for a particular effect: An Iraqi truck driver reported that Saddam Hussein had nuclear weapons; therefore, Saddam Hussein is a threat to world security. More causes are needed to prove the conclusion.

An example of ignoring the possibility of more than one possible cause: John Brown was caught out in a thunderstorm and his clothes were wet before he was rescued; therefore, he developed influenza the next day was because he got wet. Being chilled may have played a role in the illness, but Brown would have had to contract the influenza virus before he would come down with it whether or not he had gotten wet.

An example of failing to make a connection between a particular cause and an effect assigned to it. Anna fell into a putrid pond on Saturday; on Monday she came down with polio; therefore, the polio was caused by the pond. This, of course, is not acceptable unless the polio virus is found in a sample of water from the pond. A connection must be proven.

Skill 11.3   Infer information from a given passage or visual message.

See Skill 11.2.

Skill 11.4   Summarize information in a given passage or visual message.

Paraphrasing is the art of rewording text. The goal is to maintain the original purpose of the statement while translating it into your own words. Your newly generated sentence can be longer or shorter than the original. Concentrate on the meaning, not on the words. Do not change concept words, special terms, or proper names. There are numerous ways to effectively paraphrase:

- Change the key words' form or part of speech. Example: "American news **coverage** is frequently **biased** in favor of Western views," becomes "When American journalists **cover** events, they often display a Western **bias**."
- Use synonyms of "relationship words." Look for a relationship word, such as **contrast, cause,** or **effect,** and replace it with a word that conveys a similar meaning, thus creating a different structure for your sentence. Example: "**Unlike** many cats, Purrdy can sit on command," becomes "Most cats are not able to be trained, **but** Purrdy can sit on command."
- Use synonyms of phrases and words. Example: "The Beatnik writers were relatively unknown at **the start of the decade**," becomes "**Around the early 1950s**, the Beatnik writers were still relatively unknown."
- Change passive voice to active voice or move phrases and modifiers. Example: "Not to be outdone by the third graders, the fourth grade class added a musical medley to their Christmas performance," becomes "The fourth grade class added a musical medley to their Christmas performance to avoid being showed up by the third graders."
- Use reversals or negatives that do not change the meaning of the sentence. Example: "That burger chain is only found in California," becomes "That burger chain is not found on the east coast."

TEACHER CERTIFICATION STUDY GUIDE

COMPETENCY 12.0 APPLY SKILLS FOR READING FOR LITERARY RESPONSE AND PERSONAL ENJOYMENT

Skill 12.1 Analyze an author's use of figurative language to convey ideas, sensory impressions, or emotional effects.

Figurative language is also called figures of speech. If all figures of speech that have ever been identified were listed, it would be a very long list. However, for purposes of analyzing poetry, a few are sufficient.

1. Simile: Direct comparison between two things. "My love is like a red-red rose."
2. Metaphor: Indirect comparison between two things. The use of a word or phrase denoting one kind of object or action in place of another to suggest a comparison between them. While poets use them extensively, they are also integral to everyday speech. For example, chairs are said to have "legs" and "arms" although we know that it's humans and other animals that have these appendages.
3. Parallelism: The arrangement of ideas in phrases, sentences, and paragraphs that balance one element with another of equal importance and similar wording. An example from Francis Bacon's *Of Studies:* "Reading maketh a full man, conference a ready man, and writing an exact man."
4. Personification: Human characteristics are attributed to an inanimate object, an abstract quality, or animal. Examples: John Bunyan wrote characters named Death, Knowledge, Giant Despair, Sloth, and Piety in his *Pilgrim's Progress*. The metaphor of an arm of a chair is a form of personification.
5. Euphemism: The substitution of an agreeable or inoffensive term for one that might offend or suggest something unpleasant. Many euphemisms are used to refer to death to avoid using the real word such as "passed away," "crossed over," or nowadays "passed."
6. Hyperbole: Deliberate exaggeration for effect or comic effect. An example from Shakespeare's *The Merchant of Venice*:
   > Why, if two gods should play some heavenly match
   > And on the wager lay two earthly women,
   > And Portia one, there must be something else
   > Pawned with the other, for the poor rude world
   > Hath not her fellow.
7. Climax: A number of phrases or sentences are arranged in ascending order of rhetorical forcefulness. Example from Melville's *Moby Dick*: All that most maddens and torments; all that stirs up the lees of things; all truth with malice in it; all that cracks the sinews and cakes the brain; all the subtle demonisms of life and thought; all evil, to crazy Ahab, were visibly personified and made practically assailable in Moby Dick.
8. Bathos: A ludicrous attempt to portray pathos—that is, to evoke pity, sympathy, or sorrow. It may result from inappropriately dignifying the commonplace, elevated language to describe something trivial, or greatly exaggerated pathos.

MIDDLE LEVEL ENGLISH

9. Oxymoron: A contradiction in terms deliberately employed for effect. It is usually seen in a qualifying adjective whose meaning is contrary to that of the noun it modifies such as wise folly.
10. Alliteration: The repetition of consonant sounds in two or more neighboring words or syllables. In its simplest form, it reinforces one or two consonant sounds. Example: Shakespeare's Sonnet #12:
When I do count the clock that tells the time.
Some poets have used more complex patterns of alliteration by creating consonants both at the beginning of words and at the beginning of stressed syllables within words. Example: Shelley's "Stanzas
Written in Dejection Near Naples:"
The City's voice itself is soft like Solitude's
11. Onomatopoeia: The naming of a thing or action by a vocal imitation of the sound associated with it such as buzz or hiss or the use of words whose sound suggests the sense. A good example: from "The Brook" by Tennyson:
>   I chatter over stony ways,
>   In little sharps and trebles,
>   I bubble into eddying bays,
>   I babble on the pebbles.
12. Malapropism: A verbal blunder in which one word is replaced by another similar in sound but different in meaning. Comes from Sheridan's Mrs. Malaprop in *The Rivals* (1775). Thinking of the geography of contiguous countries, she spoke of the "geometry" of "contagious countries."

Poets use figures of speech to sharpen the effect and meaning of their poems and to help readers see things in ways they have never seen them before. Marianne Moore observed that a fir tree has "an emerald turkey-foot at the top." Her poem makes us aware of something we probably had never noticed before. The sudden recognition of the likeness yields pleasure in the reading. Figurative language allows for the statement of truths that more literal language cannot. Skillfully used, a figure of speech will help the reader see more clearly and to focus upon particulars. Figures of speech add many dimensions of richness to our reading and understanding of a poem; they also allow many opportunities for worthwhile analysis. The approach to take in analyzing a poem on the basis of its figures of speech is to ask the question: What does it do for the poem? Does it underscore meaning? Does it intensify understanding? Does it increase the intensity of our response?

Skill 12.2   Interpret the use of rhythm, rhyme, or imagery to evoke a response in the reader.

- **Rhythm:** Writing can be compared to dancing, in that it is a balance between words and flow. Rhythm refers to the harmony between the words chosen and the smoothness, rapidity, or disjointedness of the way those words are written. Sentences that are too long may disrupt the rhythm of a piece. Reading text out loud is an easy way to impart understanding of literary rhythm.

- **Rhyme:** Writing with rhyme can be especially effective on reader response. Think about the success Dr. Seuss had with his rhyming style. Rhyme is tricky though; used ineffectively or unnecessarily, it can break up the entire rhythm of the piece or fog the reader's understanding of it. Rhyme should be used when it is purely beneficial to the format of the piece. Make sure it is not forcing you to use more words than needed, and that each verse is moving the story forward.
- **Diction:** Diction is simply the right word in the right spot for the right purpose. The hallmark of a great writer is precise, unusual, and memorable diction.
- **Imagery:** Imagery involves engaging one or more of your five senses in your writing. An author might use imagery to give the reader a greater, more real picture of the scene they are trying to depict. Imagery may conjure up a past experience that the reader had (the smell of the ocean, the feeling of their childhood blanket) thereby enriching their mental picture of the scene.

Skill 12.3   Analyze the use of language to portray character, develop plot, or create a mood in a given passage.

It's no accident that **plot** is sometimes called action. If the plot does not *move*, the story quickly dies. Therefore, the successful writer of stories uses a wide variety of active verbs in creative and unusual ways. If a reader is kept on his/her toes by the movement of the story, the experience of reading it will be pleasurable. That reader will probably want to read more of this author's work. Careful, unique, and unusual choices of active verbs will bring about that effect. William Faulkner is a good example of a successful writer whose stories are lively and memorable because of his use of unusual active verbs. In analyzing the development of plot, it's wise to look at the verbs. However, the development of believable conflicts is also vital. If there is no conflict, there is no story. What devices does a writer use to develop the conflicts, and are they real and believable?

Character is portrayed in many ways: description of physical characteristics, dialogue, interior monologue, the thoughts of the character, the attitudes of other characters toward this one, etc. Descriptive language depends on the ability to recreate a sensory experience for the reader. If the description of the character's appearance is a visual one, then the reader must be able to *see* the character. What's the shape of the nose? What color are the eyes? How tall or how short is this character? Thin or chubby? How does the character move? How does the character walk? Terms must be chosen that will create a picture for the reader. It's not enough to say the eyes are blue, for example. What blue? Often the color of eyes is compared to something else to enhance the readers' ability to visualize the character. A good test of characterization is the level of emotional involvement of the reader in the character. If the reader is to become involved, the description must provide an actual experience—seeing, smelling, hearing, tasting, or feeling.

Dialogue will reflect characteristics. Is it clipped? Is it highly dialectal? Does a character use a lot of colloquialisms? The ability to portray the speech of a character can make or break a story. The kind of person the character is in the mind of the reader is dependent on impressions created by description and dialogue. How do other characters feel about this one as revealed by their treatment of him/her, their discussions of him/her with each other, or their overt descriptions of the character. For example, "John, of course, can't be trusted with another person's possessions." In analyzing a story, it's useful to discuss the devices used to produce character.

Setting may be visual, temporal, psychological, or social. Descriptive words are often used here also. In Edgar Allan Poe's description of the house in "The Fall of the House of Usher" as the protagonist/narrator approaches it, the air of dread and gloom that pervades the story is caught in the setting and sets the stage for the story. A setting may also be symbolic, as it is in Poe's story, where the house is a symbol of the family that lives in it. As the house disintegrates, so does the family.

The language used in all of these aspects of a story—plot, character, and setting—work together to create the **mood** of a story. Poe's first sentence establishes the mood of the story: "During the whole of a dull, dark, and soundless day in the autumn of the year, when the clouds hung oppressively low in the heavens, I had been passing alone, on horseback, through a singularly dreary tract of country; and at length found myself, as the shades of the evening drew on, within view of the melancholy House of Usher."

COMPETENCY 13.0 APPLY SKILLS FOR READING AND VIEWING FOR CRITICAL ANALYSIS AND EVALUATION

Skill 13.1 Distinguish between fact and opinion in a written or visual message.

Facts are statements that are verifiable. Opinions are statements that must be supported in order to be accepted. Facts are used to support opinions. For example, "Jane is a bad girl" is an opinion. However, "Jane hit her sister with a baseball bat" is a *fact* upon which the opinion is based. Judgments are opinions—decisions or declarations based on observation or reasoning that express approval or disapproval. Facts report what has happened or exists and come from observation, measurement, or calculation. Facts can be tested and verified whereas opinions and judgments cannot. They can only be supported with facts.

Most statements cannot be so clearly distinguished. "I believe that Jane is a bad girl" is a fact. The speaker knows what he/she believes. However, it obviously includes a judgment that could be disputed by another person who might believe otherwise. Judgments are not usually so firm. They are, rather, plausible opinions that provoke thought or lead to factual development.

Conclusions are drawn as a result of a line of reasoning. Inductive reasoning begins with particulars and reasons to a generality. For example: "When I was a child, I bit into a green apple from my grandfather's orchard, and it was sour" (specific fact #1). "I once bought green apples from a roadside vendor, and when I bit into one, it was sour" (specific fact #2). "My grocery store had a sale on green Granny Smith apples last week, and I bought several only to find that they were sour when I bit into one" (specific fact #3). Conclusion: All green apples are sour. While this is an example of inductive reasoning, it is also an example of the weakness of such reasoning. The speaker has not tasted all the green apples in the world, and there very well may be some apples that are green that are not sour.

Deductive reasoning begins with the generalization: "Green apples are sour" and supports that generalization with the specifics.

An inference is drawn from an inductive line of reasoning. The most famous one is "all men are mortal," which is drawn from the observation that everyone a person knows has died or will die and that everyone else concurs in that judgment. It is assumed to be true and for that reason can be used as proof of another conclusion: "Socrates is a man; therefore, he will die."

Sometimes the inference is assumed to be proven when it is not reliably true in all cases, such as "aging brings physical and mental infirmity." Reasoning from that *inference*, many companies will not hire anyone above a certain age. Actually, being old does not necessarily imply physical and/or mental impairment.

There are many instances where elderly people have made important contributions that require exceptional ability.

Skill 13.2　Judge the relevance, importance, or sufficiency of facts or examples in a writer's argument.

An argument is a generalization that is proven or supported with facts. If the facts are not accurate, the generalization remains unproven. Using inaccurate "facts" to support an argument is called a *fallacy* in reasoning. Some factors to consider in judging whether the facts used to support an argument are accurate are as follow:

1. Are the facts current or are they out of date? For example, if the proposition "birth defects in babies born to drug-using mothers are increasing," then the data must include the latest that is available.
2. Another important factor to consider in judging the accuracy of a fact is its source. Where was the data obtained, and is that source reliable?
3. The calculations on which the facts are based may be unreliable. It's a good idea to run one's own calculations before using a piece of derived information.

Even facts that are true and have a sharp impact on the argument may not be relevant to the case at hand.

1. Health statistics from an entire state may have no relevance, or little relevance, to a particular county or zip code. Statistics from an entire country cannot be used to prove very much about a particular state or county.
2. An analogy can be useful in making a point, but the comparison must match up in all characteristics or it will not be relevant. Analogy should be used very carefully. It is often just as likely to destroy an argument as it is to strengthen it.

The importance or significance of a fact may not be sufficient to strengthen an argument. For example, of the millions of immigrants in the U.S., using a single family to support a solution to the immigration problem will not make much difference overall even though those single-example arguments are often used to support one approach or another. They may achieve a positive reaction, but they will not prove that one solution is better than another. If enough cases were cited from a variety of geographical locations, the information might be significant.

How much is enough? Generally speaking, three strong supporting facts are sufficient to establish the thesis of an argument. For example:

Conclusion: All green apples are sour.

- When I was a child, I bit into a green apple from my grandfather's orchard, and it was sour.
- I once bought green apples from a roadside vendor, and when I bit into one, it was sour.
- My grocery store had a sale on green Granny Smith apples last week, and I bought several only to find that they were sour when I bit into one.

The fallacy in the above argument is that the sample was insufficient. A more exhaustive search of literature, etc., will probably turn up some green apples that are not sour.

Sometimes more than three arguments are too many. On the other hand, it's not unusual to hear public speakers, particularly politicians, who will cite a long litany of facts to support their positions.

Skill 13.3 Assess the objectivity or credibility of various sources of information.

Before accepting as gospel anything that is printed in a newspaper or advertising or presented on radio, television, or the Internet, it is wise to first of all consider the source. Even though news reporters and editors claim to be unbiased in the presentation of news, they usually take an editorial point of view. A newspaper may avow that it is Republican or conservative and may even make recommendations at election time, but it will still claim to present the news without bias. Sometimes this is true, and sometimes it is not. For example, Fox News declares itself to be conservative and to support the Republican party. Its presentation of news often reveals that bias. When Vice President Cheney made a statement about his shooting of a friend in a duck-hunting accident, it was only made available to Fox News.

On the other hand, CBS has tended to favor more liberal politicians although it avows that it is even-handed in its coverage. Dan Rather presented a story critical of President Bush's military service that was based on a document that could not be validated. His failure to play by the rules of certification of evidence cost him his job and his career. Even with authentication, such a story would not have gotten past the editors of a conservative-leaning news system.

Even politicians usually play by the rules of fairness in the choices they make about going public. They usually try to be even-handed. However, some channels and networks will show deference to one politician over another.

Advertising, whether in print or electronic media is another thing. Will using a certain tooth paste improve a person's love life? Is a dish better than cable? The best recourse a reader/viewer has is to ask around and find someone who has experience that is relevant or conduct research and conduct interviews of users of both.

Skill 13.4 Determine how an author uses tone and style to present a particular point of view.

A piece of writing is an integrated whole. It's not enough to just look at the various parts; the total entity must be examined. It should be considered in two ways:
- As an emotional expression of the author
- As an artistic embodiment of a meaning or set of meanings.

This is what is sometimes called "**tone**" in literary criticism.

It's important to remember that the writer is a human being with his/her own individual bents, prejudices, and emotions. A writer is telling the readers about the world as he/she sees it and will give voice to certain phases of his/her own personality. By reading a writer's works, we can know the personal qualities and emotions of the writer embodied in the work itself. However, it's important to remember that not all the writer's characteristics will be revealed in a single work. People change and may have very different attitudes at different times in their lives. Sometimes, a writer will be influenced by a desire to have a piece of work accepted or to appear to be current or by the interests and desires of the readers he/she hopes to attract. It can destroy a work or make it less than it might be. Sometimes the best works are not commercial successes in the generation when they were written but are discovered at a later time and by another generation.

There are three places to look for tone:
- Choice of form: tragedy or comedy; melodrama or farce; parody or sober lyric.
- Choice of materials: characters that have human qualities that are attractive; others that are repugnant. What an author shows in a setting will often indicate what his/her interests are.
- The writer's interpretation: it may be explicit—telling us how he/she feels.
- The writer's implicit interpretations: the author's feelings for a character come through in the description. For example, the use of "smirked" instead of "laughed"; "minced," "stalked," "marched," instead of walked.

The reader is asked to join the writer in the feelings expressed about the world and the things that happen in it. The tone of a piece of writing is important in a critical review of it.

Style, in literature, means a distinctive manner of expression and applies to all levels of language, beginning at the phonemic level—word choices, alliteration, assonance, etc.; the syntactic level—length of sentences, choice of structure and phraseology, patterns, etc.; and extends even beyond the sentence to paragraphs and chapters. What is distinctive about this writer's use of these elements?

In Steinbeck's *Grapes of Wrath*, for instance, the style is quite simple in the narrative sections and the dialogue is dialectal.

Because the emphasis is on the story—the narrative—his style is straightforward, for the most part. He just tells the story.

However, there are inter chapters where he varies his style. He uses symbols and combines them with description that is realistic. He sometimes shifts to a crisp, repetitive pattern to underscore the beeping and speeding of cars. By contrast, some of those inter chapters are lyrical, almost poetic.

These shifts in style reflect the attitude of the author toward the subject matter. He intends to make a statement, and he uses a variety of styles to strengthen the point.

COMPETENCY 14.0 UNDERSTAND THE USE OF READING STRATEGIES AND METACOGNITIVE TECHNIQUES TO CONSTRUCT MEANING AND AID COMPREHENSION

Skill 14.1 Demonstrate knowledge of strategies to use before reading to enhance comprehension.

Before reading
- Incorporate prior knowledge: Draw a connection between students' previous experiences – both personal and educational – and the topic at hand. A student who has helped out in the family garden, for example, will have a visual and basic vocabulary starting point for the study of plant physiology.
- Make predictions about what will be learned: Encourage students to identify what they think they will learn from the text, based on cues in the material (e.g., book titles, chapter headings, pictures, etc.)
- Prepare questions: Write specific questions to be answered during reading.

Skill 14.2 Demonstrate knowledge of strategies to use during reading to enhance comprehension.

During reading:
- Use context cues: Utilize other words and concepts in the same sentence or paragraph to determine the meaning of an unfamiliar word.
- Reread challenging text: Practice rereading a selection of text to check for understanding.
- Use visualizing techniques: Mental pictures formed during the reading of text can aid in comprehension and retention of information. Read alouds, followed by a discussion of how these mental pictures factually reflect the text, provide opportunity for practicing and reinforcing this technique at all grade levels.
- Make inferences: Much of human communication relies on our ability to "read between the lines" of explicit statements and make logical guesses that fill in the blanks of information not provided. Similarly, for textbooks, making inferences means making connections to information extending beyond the text and subject matter at hand. For example, a geography book making the simple declaration that Brazil has a tropical climate can allow the student to deduce a wealth of information not stated in the text (e.g., tropical climates have warm year-round temperatures and high precipitation levels, therefore certain crops will grow quite successfully and can positively impact the local economy, etc.)
- Check the predictions made before reading: Use the text to confirm earlier predictions about content, and answer the questions posed prior to reading.

Skill 14.3   Distinguish different levels of comprehension.

The question to be asked first when approaching a reading task is what is my objective? What do I want to achieve from this reading? How will I use the information I gain from this reading? Do I only need to grasp the gist of the piece? Do I need to know the line of reasoning—not only the thesis but the subpoints? Will I be reporting important and significant details orally or in a written document?

A written document can be expected to have a thesis—either expressed or derived. To discover the thesis, the reader needs to ask what point the writer intended to make? The writing can also be expected to be organized in some logical way and to have subpoints that support or establish that the thesis is valid. It is also reasonable to expect that there will be details or examples that will support the subpoints. Knowing this, the reader can make a decision about reading techniques required for the purpose that has already been established.

If the reader only needs to know the gist of a written document, speed-reading skimming techniques may be sufficient by using the forefinger, moving the eyes down the page, picking up the important statements in each paragraph and deducing mentally that this piece is about such-and-such. If the reader needs to get a little better grasp of how the writer achieved his/her purpose in the document, a quick and cursory glance—a skimming—of each paragraph will yield what the subpoints are, the topic sentences of the paragraphs, and how the thesis is developed, yielding a greater understanding of the author's purpose and method of development.

In-depth reading requires the scrutiny of each phrase and sentence with care, looking for the thesis first of all and then the topic sentences in the paragraphs that provide the development of the thesis, also looking for connections such as transitional devices that provide clues to the direction the reasoning is taking.

Sometimes rereading is necessary in order to make use of a piece of writing for an oral or written report upon a document. If this is the purpose of reading it, the first reading should provide a map for the rereading or second reading. The second time through should follow this map, and those points that are going to be used in a report or analysis will be focused upon on more carefully. Some new understandings may occur in this rereading, and it may become apparent that the "map" that was derived from the first reading will need to be adjusted. If this rereading is for the purpose of writing an analysis or using material for a report, either highlighting or note-taking is advisable.

Skill 14.4 Analyze strategies used to determine word meanings.

Identification of common morphemes, prefixes, and suffixes

This aspect of vocabulary development is to help students look for structural elements within words which they can use independently to help them determine meaning.

The terms listed below are generally recognized as the key structural analysis components.

Root words: A root word is a word from which another word is developed. The second word can be said to have its "root" in the first. This structural component nicely lends itself to a tree with roots illustration which can concretize the meaning for students. Students may also want to literally construct root words using cardboard trees and/or actual roots from plants to create word family models. This is a lovely way to help students own their root words.

Base words: A stand-alone linguistic unit which can not be deconstructed or broken down into smaller words. For example, in the word "re-tell," the base word is "tell."

Contractions: These are shortened forms of two words in which a letter or letters have been deleted. These deleted letter have been replaced by an apostrophe.

Prefixes: These are beginning units of meaning which can be added (the vocabulary word for this type of structural adding is "affixed") to a base word or root word. They can not stand alone. They are also sometimes known as "bound morphemes," meaning that they can not stand alone as a base word.

Suffixes: These are ending units of meaning which can be "affixed" or added on to the ends of root or base words. Suffixes transform the original meanings of base and root words. Like prefixes, they are also known as "bound morphemes," because they can not stand alone as words.

Compound words: Occur when two or more base words are connected to form a new word. The meaning of the new word is in some way connected with that of the base word.

Inflectional endings: Are types are suffixes that impart a new meaning to the base or root word. These endings in particular change the gender, number, tense, or form of the base or root words. Just like other suffixes, these are also termed "bound morphemes."

TEACHER CERTIFICATION STUDY GUIDE

DOMAIN IV. LITERATURE

COMPETENCY 15.0 UNDERSTAND GENRES OF FICTION AND DRAMA AND THEIR CHARACTERISTIC FEATURES

Skill 15.1 Analyze elements of fiction in passage context.

Essential terminology and literary devices germane to literary analysis include alliteration, allusion, antithesis, aphorism, apostrophe, assonance, blank verse, caesura, conceit, connotation, consonance, couplet, denotation, diction, epiphany, exposition, figurative language, free verse, hyperbole, iambic pentameter, inversion, irony, kenning, metaphor, metaphysical poetry, metonymy, motif, onomatopoeia, octava rima, oxymoron, paradox, parallelism personification, quatrain, scansion, simile, soliloquy, Spenserian stanza, synecdoche, terza rima, tone, and wit.

The more basic terms and devices, such as alliteration, allusion, analogy, aside, assonance, atmosphere, climax, consonance, denouement, elegy, foil, foreshadowing, metaphor, simile, setting, symbol, and theme are defined and exemplified in the English 5-9 Study Guide.

Antithesis: Balanced writing about conflicting ideas, usually expressed in sentence form. Some examples are expanding from the center, shedding old habits, and searching never finding.

Aphorism: A focused, succinct expression about life from a sagacious viewpoint. Writings by Ben Franklin, Sir Francis Bacon, and Alexander Pope contain many aphorisms. "Whatever is begun in anger ends in shame" is an aphorism.

Apostrophe: Literary device of addressing an absent or dead person, an abstract idea, or an inanimate object. Sonneteers, such as Sir Thomas Wyatt, John Keats, and William Wordsworth, address the moon, stars, and the dead Milton. For example, in William Shakespeare's *Julius Caesar*, Mark Antony addresses the corpse of Caesar in the speech that begins: "O, pardon me, thou bleeding piece of earth, That I am meek and gentle with these butchers! Thou art the ruins of the noblest man That ever lived in the tide of times. Woe to the hand that shed this costly blood!"

Blank Verse: Poetry written in iambic pentameter but unrhymed. Works by Shakespeare and Milton are epitomes of blank verse. Milton's Paradise Lost states, "Illumine, what is low raise and support, That to the highth of this great argument I may assert Eternal Providence And justify the ways of God to men."

Caesura: A pause, usually signaled by punctuation, in a line of poetry. The earliest usage occurs in *Beowulf*, the first English epic dating from the Anglo-Saxon era. 'To err is human, // to forgive, divine' (Pope).

Conceit: A comparison, usually in verse, between seemingly disparate objects or concepts. John Donne's metaphysical poetry contains many clever conceits. For instance, Donne's "The Flea" (1633) compares a flea bite to the act of love; and in "A Valediction: Forbidding Mourning" (1633) separated lovers are likened to the legs of a compass, the leg drawing the circle eventually returning home to "the fixed foot."

Connotation: The ripple effect surrounding the implications and associations of a given word, distinct from the denotative, or literal meaning. For example, "Good night, sweet prince, and flights of angels sing thee to thy rest," refers to a burial.

Consonance: The repeated usage of similar consonant sounds, most often used in poetry. "Sally sat sifting seashells by the seashore" is a familiar example.

Couplet: Two rhyming lines of poetry. Shakespeare's sonnets end in heroic couplets written in iambic pentameter. Pope is also a master of the couplet. His *Rape of the Lock* is written entirely in heroic couplets.

Denotation: What a word literally means, as opposed to its connotative meaning. For example, "Good night, sweet prince, and flights of angels sing thee to thy *rest*" refers to sleep.

Diction: The right word in the right spot for the right purpose. The hallmark of a great writer is precise, unusual, and memorable diction.

Epiphany: The moment when the proverbial light bulb goes off in one's head and comprehension sets in.

Exposition: Fill-in or background information about characters meant to clarify and add to the narrative; the initial plot element which precedes the buildup of conflict.

Figurative Language: Not meant in a literal sense, but to be interpreted through symbolism. Figurative language is made up of such literary devices as hyperbole, metonymy, synecdoche, and oxymoron. A synecdoche is a figure of speech in which the word for part of something is used to mean the whole; for example, "sail" for "boat," or vice versa.

Free Verse: Poetry that does not have any predictable meter or patterning. Margaret Atwood, e. e. cummings, and Ted Hughes write in this form.

Hyperbole: Exaggeration for a specific effect. For example, "I'm so hungry that I could eat a million of these."

Iambic Pentameter: The two elements in a set five-foot line of poetry. An iamb is two syllables, unaccented and accented, per foot or measure. Pentameter means five feet of these iambs per line or ten syllables.

Inversion: A typical sentence order to create a given effect or interest. Bacon's and Milton's work use inversion successfully. Emily Dickinson was fond of arranging words outside of their familiar order. For example in "Chartless" she writes "Yet know I how the heather looks" and "Yet certain am I of the spot." Instead of saying "Yet I know" and "Yet I am certain" she reverses the usual order and shifts the emphasis to the more important words.

Irony: An unexpected disparity between what is written or stated and what is really meant or implied by the author. Verbal, situational, and dramatic are the three literary ironies. Verbal irony is when an author says one thing and means something else. Dramatic irony is when an audience perceives something that a character in the literature does not know. Irony of situation is a discrepancy between the expected result and actual results. Shakespeare's plays contain numerous and highly effective use of irony. O. Henry's short stories have ironic endings.

Kenning: Another way to describe a person, place, or thing so as to avoid prosaic repetition. The earliest examples can be found in Anglo-Saxon literature such as *Beowulf* and "The Seafarer." Instead of writing King Hrothgar, the anonymous monk wrote, great Ring-Giver, or Father of his people. A lake becomes the swans' way, and the ocean or sea becomes the great whale's way. In ancient Greek literature, this device was called an "epithet."

Metaphysical Poetry: Verse characterization by ingenious wit, unparalleled imagery, and clever conceits. The greatest metaphysical poet is John Donne. Henry Vaughn and other 17th century British poets contributed to this movement as in *Words*, "I saw eternity the other night, like a great being of pure and endless light."

Metonymy: Use of an object or idea closely identified with another object or idea to represent the second. "Hit the books" means "go study." Washington, D.C. means the U.S. government and the White House means the U.S. President.

Motif: A key, oft-repeated phrase, name, or idea in a literary work. Dorset/Wessex in Hardy's novels and the moors and the harsh weather in the Bronte sisters' novels are effective use of motifs. Shakespeare's *Romeo and Juliet* represents the ill-fated young lovers' motif.

Onomatopoeia: Word used to evoke the sound in its meaning. The early Batman series used *pow, zap, whop, zonk* and *eek* in an onomatopoetic way.

Octava rima: A specific eight-line stanza of poetry whose rhyme scheme is abababcc. Lord Byron's mock epic, *Don Juan*, is written in this poetic way.

Oxymoron: A contradictory form of speech, such as jumbo shrimp, unkindly kind, or singer John Mellencamp's "It hurts so good."

Paradox: Seemingly untrue statement, which when examined more closely proves to be true. John Donne's sonnet "Death Be Not Proud" postulates that death shall die and humans will triumph over death, at first thought not true, but ultimately explained and proven in this sonnet.

Parallelism: A type of close repetition of clauses or phrases that emphasize key topics or ideas in writing. The psalms in the King James Version of the *Bible* contain many examples.

Personification: Giving human characteristics to inanimate objects or concepts. Great writers, with few exceptions, are masters of this literary device.

Quatrain: A poetic stanza composed of four lines. A Shakespearean or Elizabethan sonnet is made up of three quatrains and ends with a heroic couplet.

Scansion: The two-part analysis of a poetic line. Count the number of syllables per line and determine where the accents fall. Divide the line into metric feet. Name the meter by the type and number of feet. Much is written about scanning poetry. Try not to inundate your students with this jargon; rather allow them to feel the power of the poets' words, ideas, and images instead.

Soliloquy: A highlighted speech, in drama, usually delivered by a major character expounding on the author's philosophy or expressing, at times, universal truths. This is done with the character alone on the stage.

Spenserian Stanza: Invented by Sir Edmund Spenser for usage in *The Fairie Queene*, his epic poem honoring Queen Elizabeth I. Each stanza consists of nine lines, eight in iambic parameter. The ninth line, called an alexandrine, has two extra syllables or one additional foot.

Sprung Rhythm: Invented and used extensively by the poet, Gerard Manley Hopkins. It consists of variable meter, which combines stressed and unstressed syllables fashioned by the author. See "Pied Beauty" or "God's Grandeur."

Stream of Consciousness: A style of writing which reflects the mental processes of the characters expressing, at times, jumbled memories, feelings, and dreams. "Big time players" in this type of expression are James Joyce, Virginia Woolf, and William Faulkner.

Terza Rima: A series of poetic stanzas utilizing the recurrent rhyme scheme of aba, bcb, cdc, ded, and so forth. The second-generation Romantic poets - Keats, Byron, Shelley, and, to a lesser degree, Yeats - used this Italian verse form, especially in their odes. Dante used this stanza in *The Divine Comedy*.

Tone: The discernible attitude inherent in an author's work regarding the subject, readership, or characters. Swift's or Pope's tone is satirical. Boswell's tone toward Johnson is admiring.

Wit: Writing of genius, keenness, and sagacity expressed through clever use of language. Alexander Pope and the Augustans wrote about and were themselves said to possess wit.

Skill 15.2   Compare the characteristics of types of fictional narratives.

The major literary genres include allegory, ballad, drama, epic, epistle, essay, fable, novel, poem, romance, and the short story.

Allegory: A story in verse or prose with characters representing virtues and vices. There are two meanings, symbolic and literal. John Bunyan's *The Pilgrim's Progress* is the most renowned of this genre.

Ballad: An *in medias res* story told or sung, usually in verse and accompanied by music. Literary devices found in ballads include the refrain, or repeated section, and incremental repetition, or anaphora, for effect. Earliest forms were anonymous folk ballads. Later forms include Coleridge's Romantic masterpiece, "The Rime of the Ancient Mariner."

Drama: Plays – comedy, modern, or tragedy - typically in five acts. Traditionalists and neoclassicists adhere to Aristotle's unities of time, place and action. Plot development is advanced via dialogue. Literary devices include asides, soliloquies and the chorus representing public opinion. Greatest of all dramatists/playwrights is William Shakespeare. Other dramaturges include Ibsen, Williams, Miller, Shaw, Stoppard, Racine, Moliére, Sophocles, Aeschylus, Euripides, and Aristophanes.

Epic: Long poem usually of book length reflecting values inherent in the generative society. Epic devices include an invocation to a Muse for inspiration, purpose for writing, universal setting, protagonist and antagonist who possess supernatural strength and acumen, and interventions of a God or the gods. Understandably, there are very few epics: Homer's *Iliad* and *Odyssey*, Virgil's *Aeneid*, Milton's *Paradise Lost*, Spenser's *The Fairie Queene*, Barrett Browning's *Aurora Leigh*, and Pope's mock-epic, *The Rape of the Lock*.

Epistle: A letter that is not always originally intended for public distribution, but due to the fame of the sender and/or recipient, becomes public domain. Paul wrote epistles that were later placed in the Bible.

Essay: Typically a limited length prose work focusing on a topic and propounding a definite point of view and authoritative tone. Great essayists include Carlyle, Lamb, DeQuincy, Emerson and Montaigne, who is credited with defining this genre.

Fable: Terse tale offering up a moral or exemplum. Chaucer's "The Nun's Priest's Tale" is a fine example of a *bete fabliau* or beast fable in which animals speak and act characteristically human, illustrating human foibles.

Legend: A traditional narrative or collection of related narratives, popularly regarded as historically factual but actually a mixture of fact and fiction.

Myth: Stories that are more or less universally shared within a culture to explain its history and traditions.

Novel: The longest form of fictional prose containing a variety of characterizations, settings, local color and regionalism. Most have complex plots, expanded description, and attention to detail. Some of the great novelists include Austin, the Brontes, Twain, Tolstoy, Hugo, Hardy, Dickens, Hawthorne, Forster, and Flaubert.

Poem: The only requirement is rhythm. Sub-genres include fixed types of literature such as the sonnet, elegy, ode, pastoral, and villanelle. Unfixed types of literature include blank verse and dramatic monologue.

Romance: A highly imaginative tale set in a fantastical realm dealing with the conflicts between heroes, villains and/or monsters. "The Knight's Tale" from Chaucer's *Canterbury Tales*, *Sir Gawain and the Green Knight* and Keats' "The Eve of St. Agnes" are prime representatives.

Short Story: Typically a terse narrative, with less developmental background about characters. May include description, author's point of view, and tone. Poe emphasized that a successful short story should create one focused impact. Considered to be great short story writers are Hemingway, Faulkner, Twain, Joyce, Shirley Jackson, Flannery O'Connor, de Maupasssant, Saki, Edgar Allen Poe, and Pushkin.

Skill 15.3   Demonstrate knowledge of types of drama and their characteristics.

Comedy: The comedic form of dramatic literature is meant to amuse, and often ends happily. It uses techniques such as satire or parody, and can take many forms, from farce to burlesque. Examples include Dante Alighieri's *The Divine Comedy,* Noel Coward's play *Private Lives,* and some of Geoffrey Chaucer's *Canterbury Tales* and William Shakespeare's plays.

Tragedy: Tragedy is comedy's other half. It is defined as a work of drama written in either prose or poetry, telling the story of a brave, noble hero who, because of some tragic character flaw, brings ruin upon himself. It is characterized by serious, poetic language that evokes pity and fear. In modern times, dramatists have tried to update its image by drawing its main characters from the middle class and showing their nobility through their nature instead of their standing. The classic example of tragedy is Sophocles' *Oedipus Rex*, while Henrik Ibsen and Arthur Miller epitomize modern tragedy.

Drama: In its most general sense, a drama is any work that is designed to be performed by actors onstage. It can also refer to the broad literary genre that includes comedy and tragedy. Contemporary usage, however, denotes drama as a work that treats serious subjects and themes but does not aim for the same grandeur as tragedy.

Drama usually deals with characters of a less stately nature than tragedy. A classical example is Sophocles' tragedy *Oedipus Rex*, while Eugene O'Neill's *The Iceman Cometh* represents modern drama.

Dramatic Monologue: A dramatic monologue is a speech given by an actor, usually intended for themselves, but with the intended audience in mind. It reveals key aspects of the character's psyche and sheds insight on the situation at hand. The audience takes the part of the silent listener, passing judgment and giving sympathy at the same time. This form was invented and used predominantly by Victorian poet Robert Browning.

Skill 15.4   Analyze elements of drama in context.

Tempo

Interpretation of dialogue must be connected to motivation and detail. During this time, the director is also concerned with pace and seeks a variation of tempo. If the overall pace is too slow, then the action becomes dull and dragging. If the overall pace is too fast, then the audience will not be able to understand what is going on, for they are being hit with too much information to process.

Dramatic Arc

Good drama is built on conflict of some kind — an opposition of forces or desires that must be resolved by the end of the story. The conflict can be internal, involving emotional and psychological pressures, or it can be external, drawing the characters into tumultuous events. These themes are presented to the audience in a narrative arc that looks roughly like this:

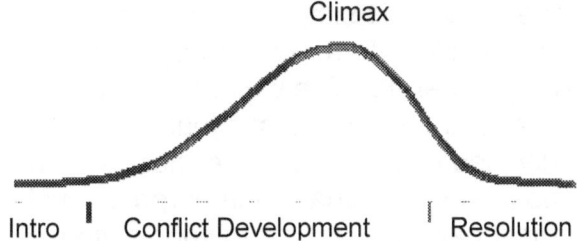

Intro | Conflict Development | Resolution

Following the Arc

Although any performance may have a series of rising and falling levels of intensity, in general the opening should set in motion the events which will generate an emotional high toward the middle or end of the story. Then, regardless of whether the ending is happy, sad, bittersweet, or despairing, the resolution eases the audience down from those heights and establishes some sense of closure. Reaching the climax too soon undermines the dramatic impact of the remaining portion of the performance, whereas reaching it too late rushes the ending and creates a jarringly abrupt end to events.

COMPTENCY 16.0 UNDERSTAND GENRES OF NONFICTION AND THEIR CHARACTERISTIC FEATURES

Skill 16.1 Compare and contrast characteristics of types of nonfiction.

Biography: A form of nonfictional literature, the subject of which is the life of an individual. The earliest biographical writings were probably funeral speeches and inscriptions, usually praising the life and example of the deceased. Early biographies evolved from this and were almost invariably uncritical, even distorted, and always laudatory. Beginning in the 18th century, this form of literature saw major development; an eminent example is James Boswell's *Life of Johnson*, which is very detailed and even records conversations. Eventually, the antithesis of the grossly exaggerated tomes praising an individual, usually a person of circumstance, developed. This form is denunciatory, debunking, and often inflammatory. A famous modern example is Lytton Strachey's *Eminent Victorians* (1918).

Autobiography: A form of biography, but it is written by the subject himself or herself. Autobiographies can range from the very formal to intimate writings made during one's life that were not intended for publication. These include letters, diaries, journals, memoirs, and reminiscences. Autobiography, generally speaking, began in the 15th century; one of the first examples is one written in England by Margery Kempe. There are four kinds of autobiography: thematic, religious, intellectual, and fictionalized. Some "novels" may be thinly disguised autobiography, such as the novels of Thomas Wolfe.

Informational books and articles: Make up much of the reading of modern Americans. Magazines began to be popular in the 19th century in this country, and while many of the contributors to those publications intended to influence the political/social/religious convictions of their readers, many also simply intended to pass on information. A book or article whose purpose is simply to be informative, that is, not to persuade, is called exposition (adjectival form: expository). An example of an expository book is the *MLA Style Manual*. The writers do not intend to persuade their readers to use the recommended stylistic features in their writing; they are simply making them available in case a reader needs such a guide. Articles in magazines such as *Time* may be persuasive in purpose, such as Joe Klein's regular column, but for the most part they are expository, giving information that television coverage of a news story might not have time to include.

Newspaper accounts of events: Expository in nature, of course, a reporting of a happening. That happening might be a school board meeting, an automobile accident that sent several people to a hospital and accounted for the death of a passenger, or the election of the mayor. They are not intended to be persuasive although the bias of a reporter or of an editor must be factored in. A newspapers' editorial stance is often openly declared, and it may be reflected in such things as news reports. Reporters are expected to be unbiased in their coverage and most of them will defend their disinterest fiercely, but what a writer *sees* in an event is inevitably shaped to some extent by the writer's beliefs and experiences.

Skill 16.2   Apply criteria for evaluating nonfiction works of various genres.

Reading emphasis in middle school

Reading for comprehension of factual material - content area textbooks, reference books, and newspapers - is closely related to study strategies in the middle/junior high. Organized study models, such as the SQ3R method, a technique that makes it possible and feasible to learn the content of even large amounts of text (Survey, Question, Read, Recite, and Review Studying), teach students to locate main ideas and supporting details, to recognize sequential order, to distinguish fact from opinion, and to determine cause/ effect relationships.

Strategies

1. Teacher-guided activities that require students to organize and to summarize information based on the author's explicit intent are pertinent strategies in middle grades. Evaluation techniques include oral and written responses to standardized or teacher-made worksheets.

2. Reading of fiction introduces and reinforces skills in inferring meaning from narration and description. Teaching-guided activities in the process of reading for meaning should be followed by cooperative planning of the skills to be studied and of the selection of reading resources. Many printed reading for comprehension instruments as well as individualized computer software programs exist to monitor the progress of acquiring comprehension skills.

3. Older middle school students should be given opportunities for more student-centered activities - individual and collaborative selection of reading choices based on student interest, small group discussions of selected works, and greater written expression. Evaluation techniques include teacher monitoring and observation of discussions and written work samples.

4. Certain students may begin some fundamental critical interpretation - recognizing fallacious reasoning in news media, examining the accuracy of news reports and advertising, explaining their reasons for preferring one author's writing to another's. Development of these skills may require a more learning-centered approach in which the teacher identifies a number of objectives and suggested resources from which the student may choose his course of study. Self-evaluation through a reading diary should be stressed. Teacher and peer evaluation of creative projects resulting from such study is encouraged.

5. Reading aloud before the entire class as a formal means of teacher evaluation should be phased out in favor of one-to-one tutoring or peer-assisted reading. Occasional sharing of favored selections by both teacher and willing students is a good oral interpretation basic.

Skill 16.3   Analyze elements of nonfiction in context.

An easy and effective way of organizing information to be used in a work of nonfiction is by asking specific questions that are geared towards a particular mode of presentation. An example of these questions follows:

Useful research questions:

What is it?

It is the process of thinking up and writing down a set of questions that you want to answer about the research topic you have selected.

Why should I do it?

It will keep you from getting lost or off-track when looking for information. You will try to find the answers to these questions when you do your research.

When do I do it?

After you have written your statement of purpose, and have a focused topic to ask questions about, begin research.

How do I do it?

Make two lists of questions. Label one "factual" questions and one "interpretive" questions. The answers to factual questions will give your reader the basic background information they need to understand your topic. The answers to interpretive questions show your creative thinking in your project and can become the basis for your thesis statement.

Asking factual questions:

Assume your reader knows nothing about your subject. Make an effort to tell them everything they need to know to understand what you will say in your project.

Make a list of specific questions that ask: Who? What? When? Where?

Example: For a report about President Abraham Lincoln's attitude and policies towards slavery, people will have to know; Who was Abraham Lincoln? Where and when was he born? What political party did he belong to? When was he elected president? What were the attitudes and laws about slavery during his lifetime? How did his actions affect slavery?

Asking Interpretive Questions:

These kinds of questions are the result of your own original thinking. They can be based on the preliminary research you have done on your chosen topic. Select one or two to answer in your presentation. They can be the basis of forming a thesis statement.

- **Hypothetical**: How would things be different today if something in the past had been different?

Example: How would our lives be different today if the Confederate (southern) states had won the United States Civil War? What would have happened to the course of World War Two if the Atomic Bomb hadn't been dropped on Hiroshima and Nagasaki?

- **Prediction**: How will something look or be in the future, based on the way it is now?

Example: What will happen to sea levels if global warming due to ozone layer depletion continues and the polar caps melt significantly? If the population of China continues to grow at the current rate for the next fifty years, how will that impact its role in world politics?

- **Solution**: What solutions can be offered to a problem that exists today?

Example: How could global warming be stopped? What can be done to stop the spread of sexually transmitted diseases among teenagers?

- **Comparison or Analogy**: Find the similarities and differences between your main subject and a similar subject, or with another subject in the same time period or place.

Example: In what ways is the Civil War in the former Yugoslavia similar to (or different from) the United States Civil War?
What is the difference in performance between a Porsche and a Lamborghini?

- **Judgment**: Based on the information you find, what can you say as your informed opinion about the subject?

Example: How does tobacco advertising affect teen cigarette smoking? What are the major causes of eating disorders among young women? How does teen parenthood affect the future lives of young women and men?

COMPETENCY 17.0 UNDERSTAND FORMS OF POETRY AND THEIR CHARACTERISTIC FEATURES

Skill 17.1 Analyze the formal characteristics and distinctive content of narrative poetry.

The greatest difficulty in analyzing narrative poetry is that it partakes of many genres. It can have all the features of poetry: meter, rhyme, verses, stanzas, etc., but it can have all the features of prose, not only fictional prose but also nonfictional. It can have a protagonist, characters, conflicts, action, plot, climax, theme, and tone. It can also be a persuasive discourse and have a thesis (real or derived) and supporting points. The arrangement of an analysis will depend to a great extent upon the peculiarities of the poem itself.

In an epic, the conflicts take place in the social sphere rather than a personal life, and it will have a historical basis or one that is accepted as historical. The conflict will be between opposed nations or races and will involve diverging views of civilization that are the foundation of the challenge. Often it will involve the pitting of a group that conceives of itself as a higher civilization against a lower civilization and, more often than not, divine will determines that the higher one will win, exerting its force over the lower, barbarous, and profane enemy. Examples are the conflict of Greece with Troy, the fates of Rome with the Carthaginian and the Italian, the Crusaders with the Saracen, or even of Milton's Omnipotent versus Satan. In analyzing these works, protagonist and antagonist need to be clearly identified, the conflicts established, the climax and an outcome that sets the world right in the mind of the writer clearly shown .

At the same time, the form of the epic as a poem must be considered. What meter, rhyme scheme, verse form, and stanza form have been chosen to tell this story. Is it consistent? If it varies, where does it vary and what does the varying do for the poem/story? What about figures of speech? Is there alliteration or onomatopoeia? Etc.

The epic is a major literary form historically although it had begun to fall out of favor by the end of the seventeenth century. There have been notable efforts to produce an American epic, but they always seem to slide over into prose. The short story and the novel began to take over the genre. Even so, some would say that *Moby Dick* is an American epic.

Narrative poetry has been very much a part of the output of modern American writers totally apart from attempts to write epics. Many of Emily Dickenson's poems are narrative in form and retain the features that we look for in the finest of American poetry. The first two verses of "A Narrow Fellow in the Grass" illustrate the use of narrative in a poem:

> A narrow fellow in the grass
> Occasionally rides;
> You may have met him—did you not?
> His notice sudden is.

> The grass divides as with a comb,
> A spotted shaft is seen;
> And then it closes at your feet
> And opens further on. . . .

This is certainly narrative in nature and has many of the aspects of prose narrative. At the same time, it is a poem with rhyme, meter, verses, stanzas, etc. and can be analyzed as such.

When we speak of *form* with regard to poetry, we usually mean one of three things:
1. The pattern of the sound and rhythm
2. The visible shape it takes
3. Rhyme or free verse

1. The pattern of the sound and rhythm

It helps to know the history of this peculiarity of poetry. History was passed down in oral form almost exclusively until the invention of the printing press and was often set to music. A rhymed story is much easier to commit to memory. Adding a tune makes it even easier to remember, so it's not a surprise that much of the earliest literature—epics, odes, etc., are rhymed and were probably sung. When we speak of the pattern of sound and rhythm, we are referring to two things: verse form and stanza form.

The verse form is the rhythmic pattern of a single verse. An example would be any meter: blank verse, for instance, is iambic pentameter. A stanza is a group of a certain number of verses (lines), having a rhyme scheme. If the poem is written, there is usually white space between the verses although a short poem may be only one stanza. If the poem is spoken, there will be a pause between stanzas.

2. The visible shape it takes

In the seventeenth century, some poets shaped their poems to reflect the theme. A good example is George Herbert's *Easter Wings*. Since that time, poets have occasionally played with this device; it is, however, generally viewed as nothing more than a demonstration of ingenuity. The rhythm, effect, and meaning are often sacrificed to the forcing of the shape.

3. Rhyme and free verse

Poets also use devices to establish form that will underscore the meanings of their poems. A very common one is alliteration. When the poem is read (which poetry is usually intended to be), the repetition of a sound may not only underscore the meaning, it may also pleasure to the reading. Following a strict rhyming pattern can add intensity to the meaning of the poem in the hands of a skilled and creative poet.

On the other hand, the meaning can be drowned out by the steady beat-beat-beat of it. Shakespeare very skillfully used the regularity of rhyme in his poetry, breaking the rhythm at certain points to very effectively underscore a point. For example, in Sonnet #130, "My mistress' eyes are nothing like the sun," the rhythm is primarily iambic pentameter. It lulls the reader (or listener) to accept that this poet is following the standard conventions for love poetry, which in that day reliably used rhyme and more often than not iambic pentameter to express feelings of romantic love along conventional lines. However, in Sonnet #130, the last two lines sharply break from the monotonous pattern, forcing reader or speaker to pause:

    And yet, by heaven, I think my love as rare
    As any she belied with false compare

Shakespeare's purpose is clear: he is not writing a conventional love poem; the object of his love is not the red-and-white conventional woman written about in other poems of the period. This is a good example where a poet uses form to underscore meaning.

Poets eventually began to feel constricted by the rhyming conventions and began to break away and make new rules for poetry. When poetry was only rhymed, it was easy to define it. When free verse, or poetry written in a flexible form, came upon the scene in France in the 1880s, it quickly began to influence English-language poets such as T. S. Eliot, whose memorable poem, *The Wasteland*, had an alarming but desolate message for the modern world. It's impossible to imagine that it could have been written in the soothing, lulling rhymed verse of previous periods. Those who first began writing in free verse in English were responding to the influence of the French *vers libre*. However, it should be noted that it could be loosely applied to the poetry of Walt Whitman, writing in the mid-nineteenth century, as can be seen in the first stanza of *Son of Myself*:

    I celebrate myself, and sing myself,
    And what I assume you shall assume,
    For every atom belonging to me as good belongs to you.

When poetry was no longer defined as a piece of writing arranged in verses that had a rhyme-scheme of some sort, distinguishing poetry from prose became a point of discussion. Merriam Webster's *Encyclopedia of Literature* defines poetry as follows: "Writing that formulates a concentrated imaginative awareness of experience in language chosen and arranged to create a specific emotional response through its meaning, sound and rhythm."

A poet chooses the form of his poetry deliberately, based upon the emotional response he hopes to evoke and the meaning he wishes to convey. Robert Frost, a twentieth-century poet who chose to use conventional rhyming verse to make his point is a memorable and often-quoted modern poet. Who can forget his closing lines in "Stopping by Woods"?

    And miles to go before I sleep,
    And miles to go before I sleep.

Would they be as memorable if the poem had been written in free verse?

Slant Rhyme: Occurs when the final consonant sounds are the same, but the vowels are different. Occurs frequently in Irish, Welsh, and Icelandic verse. Examples include: green and gone, that and hit, ill and shell.

Alliteration: Alliteration occurs when the initial sounds of a word, beginning either with a consonant or a vowel, are repeated in close succession. Examples include: Athena and Apollo, Nate never knows, People who pen poetry.

Note that the words only have to be close to one another: Alliteration that repeats and attempts to connect a number of words is little more than a tongue-twister.

The function of alliteration, like rhyme, might be to accentuate the beauty of language in a given context, or to unite words or concepts through a kind of repetition. Alliteration, like rhyme, can follow specific patterns. Sometimes the consonants aren't always the initial ones, but they are generally the stressed syllables. Alliteration is less common than rhyme, but because it is less common, it can call our attention to a word or line in a poem that might not have the same emphasis otherwise.

Assonance: If alliteration occurs at the beginning of a word and rhyme at the end, assonance takes the middle territory. Assonance occurs when the vowel sound within a word matches the same sound in a nearby word, but the surrounding consonant sounds are different. "Tune" and "June" are rhymes; "tune" and "food" are assonant. The function of assonance is frequently the same as end rhyme or alliteration; all serve to give a sense of continuity or fluidity to the verse. Assonance might be especially effective when rhyme is absent: It gives the poet more flexibility, and it is not typically used as part of a predetermined pattern. Like alliteration, it does not so much determine the structure or form of a poem; rather, it is more ornamental.

Onomatopoeia: Word used to evoke the sound in its meaning. The early Batman series used *pow*, *zap*, *whop*, *zonk* and *eek* in an onomatopoetic way.

Rhythm in poetry refers to the recurrence of stresses at equal intervals. A stress (accent) is a greater amount of force given to one syllable in speaking than is given to another. For example, we put the stress on the first syllable of such words as father, mother, daughter, children. The unstressed or unaccented syllable is sometimes called a slack syllable. All English words carry at least one stress except articles and some prepositions such as by, from, at, etc. Indicating where stresses occur is to scan; doing this is called scansion. Very little is gained in understanding a poem or making a statement about it by merely scanning it. The pattern of the rhythm—the meter—should be analyzed in terms of its overall relationship to the message and impression of the poem.

Slack syllables, when they recur in pairs cause rhythmic trippings and bouncings; on the other hand, recurrent pairs of stresses will create a heavier rocking effect. The rhythm is dependent on words to convey meaning. Alone, they communicate nothing.

When examining the rhythm and meaning of a poem, a good question to ask is whether the rhythm is appropriate to the theme. A bouncing rhythm, for example, might be dissonant in a solemn elegy.

Stops are those places in a poem where the punctuation requires a pause. An end-stopped line is one that *ends* in a pause whereas one that has no punctuation at its end and is, therefore, read with only a slight pause after it is said to be run-on and the running on of its thought into the next line is called enjambment. These are used by a poet to underscore, intensify, communicate meaning.

Rhythm, then, is a *pattern of recurrence* and in poetry is made up of stressed and relatively unstressed syllables. The poet can manipulate the rhythm by making the intervals between his stresses regular or varied, by making his lines short or long, by end-stopping his lines or running them over, by choosing words that are easier or less easy to say, by choosing polysyllabic words or monosyllables. The most important thing to remember about rhythm is that it conveys meaning.

The basic unit of rhythm is called a foot and is usually one stressed syllable with one or two unstressed ones or two stressed syllables with one unstressed one. A foot made up of one unstressed syllable and one stressed one is called an iamb. If a line is made of five iambs, it is iambic pentameter. A rhymed poem typically establishes a pattern such as iambic pentameter, and even though there will be syllables that don't fit the pattern, the poem, nevertheless, will be said to be in iambic pentameter. In fact, a poem may be considered weak if the rhythm is too monotonous.

The most common kinds of feet in English poetry:

iamb: -'
anapest: --'
trochee: '-
dactyl: '--
Monosyllabic: '
Spondee: "
Pyrrhic foot: --

Iambic and anapestic are said to be rising because the movement is from slack to stressed syllables. Trochaic and dactylic are said to be falling.

Meters are named as follows:
Monometer: a line of one foot
Dimeter: a line of two feet
Trimeter: a line of three feet
Tetrameter: a line of four feet
Pentameter: a line of five feet
Hexameter: a line of six feet
Heptameter: a line of seven feet

Octameter: a line of eight feet

Longer lines are possible, but a reader will tend to break it up into shorter lengths.

A caesura is a definite pause within a line, in scansion indicated by a double line: ||

A stanza is a group of a certain number of lines with a rhyme scheme or a particular rhythm or both, typically set off by white space.

Some typical patterns of English poetry:
Blank verse: unrhymed iambic pentameter.
Couplet: two-line stanza, usually rhymed and typically not separated by white space.
Heroic couplet or closed couplet: two rhymed lines of iambic pentameter, the first ending in a light pause, the second more heavily end-stopped.
Tercet: a three-line stanza, which, if rhymed, usually keeps to one rhyme sound.
Terza rima: the middle line of the tercet rhymes with the first and third lines of the next tercet.
The quatrain: four-line stanza, the most popular in English.
The ballad stanza: four iambic feet in lines 1 and 3, three in lines 2 and 4. Rhyming is abcb.
The refrain: a line or lines repeated in a ballad as a chorus.
Terminal refrain: follows a stanza in a ballad.
Five-line stanzas occur, but not frequently.
Six-line stanzas, more frequent than five-line ones.
The sestina: six six-line stanzas and a tercet. Repeats in each stanza the same six end-words in a different order.
Rime royal: seven-line stanza in iambic pentameter with rhyme ababbcc.
Ottava rima: eight-line stanza of iambic pentameter rhyming abababcc.
Spenserian stanza: nine lines, rhyming ababbcbcc for eight lines then concludes with an Alexandrine.
The Alexandrine: a line of iambic hexameter.
Free verse: no conventional patterns of rhyme, stanza, or meter.
Sonnet: a fourteen-line poem in iambic pentameter.
1) English sonnet: sometimes called a Shakespearean sonnet. Rhymes cohere in four clusters: abab cdcd efef gg
2) Italian or Petrarchan sonnet: first eight lines (the octave), abbaabba; then the sestet, the last six lines add new rhyme sounds in almost any variation; does not end in a couplet.

Skill 17.2 Relate various types of lyric poetry to their formal characteristics.

The sonnet is a fixed-verse form of Italian origin, which consists of 14 lines that are typically five-foot iambics rhyming according to a prescribed scheme. Popular since its creation in the thirteenth century in Sicily, it spread at first to Tuscany, where it was adopted by Petrarch.

The Petrarchan sonnet generally has a two-part theme. The first eight lines, the octave, state a problem, ask a question, or express an emotional tension. The last six lines, the sestet, resolve the problem, answer the question, or relieve the tension. The rhyme scheme of the octave is abbaabba; that of the sestet varies.

Sir Thomas Wyatt and Henry Howard, Earl of Surrey, introduced this form into England in the sixteenth century. It played an important role in the development of Elizabethan lyric poetry, and a distinctive English sonnet developed, which was composed of three quatrains, each with an independent rhyme-scheme, and it ended with a rhymed couplet. A form of the English sonnet created by Edmond Spenser combines the English form and the Italian. The Spenserian sonnet follows the English quatrain and couplet pattern but resembles the Italian in its rhyme scheme, which is linked: abab bcbc cdcd ee. Many poets wrote sonnet sequences, where several sonnets were linked together, usually to tell a story. Considered to be the greatest of all sonnet sequences is one of Shakespeare's, which are addressed to a young man and a "dark lady" wherein the love story is overshadowed by the underlying reflections on time and art, growth and decay, and fame and fortune.

The sonnet continued to develop, more in topics than in form. When John Donne in the seventeenth century used the form for religious themes, some of which are almost sermons, or on personal reflections ("When I consider how my light is spent"), there were no longer any boundaries on the themes it could take.

That it is a flexible form is demonstrated in the wide range of themes and purposes it has been used for—all the way from more frivolous concerns to statements about time and death. Wordsworth, Keats, and Elizabeth Barrett Browning used the Petrarchan form of the sonnet. A well-known example is Wordsworth's "The World Is Too Much With Us." Rainer Maria Rilke's Sonnette an Orpheus (1922) is a well-known twentieth-century sonnet.

Analysis of a sonnet should focus on the form—does it fit a traditional pattern or does it break from tradition? If so, why did the poet choose to make that break? Does it reflect the purpose of the poem? What is the theme? What is the purpose? Is it narrative? If so, what story does it tell and is there an underlying meaning? Is the sonnet appropriate for the subject matter?

The limerick probably originated in County Limerick, Ireland, in the 18th century. It is a form of short, humorous verse, often nonsensical, and often ribald. Its five lines rhyme aabbaa with three feet in all lines except the third and fourth, which have only two. Rarely presented as serious poetry, this form is popular because almost anyone can write it.

Analysis of a limerick should focus on its form. Does it conform to a traditional pattern or does it break from the tradition? If so, what impact does that have on the meaning? Is the poem serious or frivolous? Is it funny? Does it try to be funny but does not achieve its purpose? Is there a serious meaning underlying the frivolity?

A cinquain is a poem with a five-line stanza. Adelaide Crapsey (1878-1914) called a five-line verse form a cinquain and invented a particular meter for it. Similar to the haiku, there are two syllables in the first and last lines and four, six, and eight in the middle three lines. It has a mostly iambic cadence. Her poem, "November Night," is an example:

> Listen...
> With faint dry sound
> Like steps of passing ghosts,
> the leaves, frost-crisp'd, break from the trees
> And fall.

Haiku is a very popular unrhymed form that is limited to seventeen syllables arranged in three lines thus: five, seven, and five syllables. This verse form originated in Japan in the seventeenth century where it is accepted as serious poetry and is Japan's most popular form. Originally, it was to deal with the season, the time of day, and the landscape although as it has come into more common use, the subjects have become less restricted. The imagist poets and other English writers used the form or imitated it. It's a form much used in classrooms to introduce students to the writing of poetry.

Analysis of a cinquain and a haiku poem should focus on form first. Does the haiku poem conform to the seventeen-syllables requirement and are they arranged in a five, seven, and five pattern? For a cinquain, does it have only five lines? Does the poem distill the words so as much meaning as possible can be conveyed? Does it treat a serious subject? Is the theme discernable? Short forms like these seem simple to dash off; however, they are not effective unless the words are chosen and pared so the meaning intended is conveyed. The impact should be forceful, and that often takes more effort, skill, and creativity than longer forms. This should be taken into account in their analysis.

Skill 17.3   Analyze elements of poetry in context.

Imagery can be described as a word or sequence of words that refers to any sensory experience—that is, anything that can be seen, tasted, smelled, heard, or felt on the skin or fingers. While writers of prose may also use these devices, it is most distinctive of poetry. The poet intends to make an experience available to the reader. In order to do that, he/she must appeal to one of the senses. The most-often-used one, of course, is the visual sense. The poet will deliberately paint a scene in such a way that the reader can see it. However, the purpose is not simply to stir the visceral feeling but also to stir the emotions. A good example is "The Piercing Chill" by Taniguchi Buson (1715-1783):

> The piercing chill I feel:
>   My dead wife's comb, in our bedroom,
>   Under my heel . . .

In only a few short words, the reader can feel many things: the shock that might come from touching the corpse, a literal sense of death, the contrast between her death and the memories he has of her when she was alive.

Imagery might be defined as speaking of the abstract in concrete terms, a powerful device in the hands of a skillful poet.

A **symbol** is an object or action that can be observed with the senses in addition to its suggesting many other things. The lion is a symbol of courage; the cross a symbol of Christianity; the color green a symbol of envy. These can almost be defined as metaphors because society pretty much agrees on the one-to-one meaning of them. Symbols used in literature are usually of a different sort. They tend to be private and personal; their significance is only evident in the context of the work where they are used. A good example is the huge pair of spectacles on a sign board in Fitzgerald's *The Great Gatsby*. They are interesting as a part of the landscape, but they also symbolize divine myopia. A symbol can certainly have more than one meaning, and the meaning may be as personal as the memories and experiences of the particular reader. In analyzing a poem or a story, it's important to identify the symbols and their possible meanings.

Looking for symbols is often challenging, especially for novice poetry readers. However, these suggestions may be useful: First, pick out all the references to concrete objects such as a newspaper, black cats, etc. Note any that the poet emphasizes by describing in detail, by repeating, or by placing at the very beginning or ending of a poem. Ask yourself, what is the poem about? What does it add up to? Paraphrase the poem and determine whether or not the meaning depends upon certain concrete objects. Then ponder what the concrete object symbolizes in this particular poem. Look for a character with the name of a prophet who does little but utter prophecy or a trio of women who resemble the Three Fates. A symbol may be a part of a person's body such as the eye of the murder victim in Poe's story *The Tell-Tale Heart* or a look, a voice, or a mannerism.

Some things a symbol is not: an abstraction such as truth, death, and love; in narrative, a well-developed character who is not at all mysterious; the second term in a metaphor. In Emily Dickenson's *The Lightning is a yellow Fork*, the symbol is the lightning, not the fork.

An **allusion** is very much like a symbol, and the two sometimes tend to run together. An allusion is defined by Merriam Webster's *Encyclopedia of Literature* as "an implied reference to a person, event, thing, or a part of another text." Allusions are based on the assumption that there is a common body of knowledge shared by poet and reader and that a reference to that body of knowledge will be immediately understood. Allusions to the Bible and classical mythology are common in western literature on the assumption that they will be immediately understood. This is not always the case, of course. T. S. Eliot's *The Wasteland* requires research and annotation for understanding. He assumed more background on the part of the average reader than actually exists.

However, when Michael Moore on his web page headlines an article on the war in Iraq: "Déjà Fallouja: Ramadi surrounded, thousands of families trapped, no electricity or water, onslaught impending," we understand immediately that he is referring first of all to a repeat of the human disaster in New Orleans although the "onslaught" is not a storm but an invasion by American and Iraqi troops.

The use of allusion is a sort of shortcut for poets. They can use an economy of words and count on meaning to come from the reader's own experience.

Figurative language is also called figures of speech. If all figures of speech that have ever been identified were listed, it would be a very long list. However, for purposes of analyzing poetry, a few are sufficient.

13. Simile: Direct comparison between two things. "My love is like a red-red rose."
14. Metaphor: Indirect comparison between two things. The use of a word or phrase denoting one kind of object or action in place of another to suggest a comparison between them. While poets use them extensively, they are also integral to everyday speech. For example, chairs are said to have "legs" and "arms" although we know that it's humans and other animals that have these appendages.
15. Parallelism: The arrangement of ideas in phrases, sentences, and paragraphs that balance one element with another of equal importance and similar wording. An example from Francis Bacon's *Of Studies*: "Reading maketh a full man, conference a ready man, and writing an exact man."
16. Personification: Human characteristics are attributed to an inanimate object, an abstract quality, or animal. Examples: John Bunyan wrote characters named Death, Knowledge, Giant Despair, Sloth, and Piety in his *Pilgrim's Progress*. The metaphor of an arm of a chair is a form of personification.
17. Euphemism: The substitution of an agreeable or inoffensive term for one that might offend or suggest something unpleasant. Many euphemisms are used to refer to death to avoid using the real word such as "passed away," "crossed over," or nowadays "passed."
18. Hyperbole: Deliberate exaggeration for effect or comic effect. An example from Shakespeare's *The Merchant of Venice*:
    Why, if two gods should play some heavenly match
    And on the wager lay two earthly women,
    And Portia one, there must be something else
    Pawned with the other, for the poor rude world
    Hath not her fellow.
19. Climax: A number of phrases or sentences are arranged in ascending order of rhetorical forcefulness. Example from Melville's *Moby Dick*: All that most maddens and torments; all that stirs up the lees of things; all truth with malice in it; all that cracks the sinews and cakes the brain; all the subtle demonisms of life and thought; all evil, to crazy Ahab, were visibly personified and made practically assailable in Moby Dick.

20. Bathos: A ludicrous attempt to portray pathos—that is, to evoke pity, sympathy, or sorrow. It may result from inappropriately dignifying the commonplace, elevated language to describe something trivial, or greatly exaggerated pathos.
21. Oxymoron: A contradiction in terms deliberately employed for effect. It is usually seen in a qualifying adjective whose meaning is contrary to that of the noun it modifies such as wise folly.
22. Irony: Expressing something other than and particularly opposite the literal meaning such as words of praise when blame is intended. In poetry, it is often used as a sophisticated or resigned awareness of contrast between what is and what ought to be and expresses a controlled pathos without sentimentality. It is a form of indirection that avoids overt praise or censure. An early example: the Greek comic character Eiron, a clever underdog who by his wit repeatedly triumphs over the boastful character Alazon.
23. Alliteration: The repetition of consonant sounds in two or more neighboring words or syllables. In its simplest form, it reinforces one or two consonant sounds. Example: Shakespeare's Sonnet #12:
    When I do count the clock that tells the time.
    Some poets have used more complex patterns of alliteration by creating consonants both at the beginning of words and at the beginning of stressed syllables within words. Example: Shelley's "Stanzas Written in Dejection Near Naples"
    The City's voice itself is soft like Solitude's
24. Onomatopoeia: The naming of a thing or action by a vocal imitation of the sound associated with it such as buzz or hiss or the use of words whose sound suggests the sense. A good example: from "The Brook" by Tennyson:
    I chatter over stony ways,
    In little sharps and trebles,
    I bubble into eddying bays,
    I babble on the pebbles.
25. Malapropism: A verbal blunder in which one word is replaced by another similar in sound but different in meaning. Comes from Sheridan's Mrs. Malaprop in *The Rivals* (1775). Thinking of the geography of contiguous countries, she spoke of the "geometry" of "contagious countries."

Poets use figures of speech to sharpen the effect and meaning of their poems and to help readers see things in ways they have never seen them before. Marianne Moore observed that a fir tree has "an emerald turkey-foot at the top." Her poem makes us aware of something we probably had never noticed before. The sudden recognition of the likeness yields pleasure in the reading. Figurative language allows for the statement of truths that more literal language cannot. Skillfully used, a figure of speech will help the reader see more clearly and to focus upon particulars. Figures of speech add many dimensions of richness to our reading and understanding of a poem; they also allow many opportunities for worthwhile analysis. The approach to take in analyzing a poem on the basis of its figures of speech is to ask the question: What does it do for the poem?
Does it underscore meaning? Does it intensify understanding? Does it increase the intensity of our response?

COMPETENCY 18.0 UNDERSTAND THE SOCIAL AND CULTURAL ASPECTS OF LITERATURE, INCLUDING THE WAYS IN WHICH LITERARY WORKS AND MOVEMENTS BOTH REFLECT AND SHAPE CULTURE AND HISTORY

Skill 18.1   Apply knowledge of the characteristics and significance of mythology and folk literature.

Literary allusions are drawn from classic mythology, national folklore, and religious writings that are supposed to have such familiarity to the reader that he can recognize the comparison between the subject of the allusion and the person, place, or event in the current reading. Children and adolescents who have knowledge of proverbs, fables, myths, epics, and the *Bible* can understand these allusions and thereby appreciate their reading to a greater degree than those who cannot recognize them.

Fables and folktales

This literary group of stories and legends was originally orally transmitted to the common populace to provide models of exemplary behavior or deeds worthy of recognition and homage.

In fables, animals talk, feel, and behave like human beings. The fable always has a moral and the animals illustrate specific people or groups without directly identifying them. For example, in Aesop's *Fables,* the lion is the "King" and the wolf is the cruel, often unfeeling, "noble class." In the fable of "The Lion and the Mouse" the moral is that "Little friends may prove to be great friends." In "The Lion's Share" it is "Might makes right." Many British folktales - *How Robin Became an Outlaw* and *St. George - Slaying of the Dragon* - stress the correlation between power and right.

Classical mythology

Much of the mythology that produces allusions in modern English writings is a product of ancient Greece and Rome because these myths have been more liberally translated. Some Norse myths are also well known. Children are fond of myths because those ancient people were seeking explanations for those elements in their lives that predated scientific knowledge just as children seek explanations for the occurrences in their lives. These stories provide insight into the order and ethics of life as ancient heroes overcome the terrors of the unknown and bring meaning to the thunder and lightning, to the changing of the seasons, to the magical creatures of the forests and seas, and to the myriad of natural phenomena that can frighten mankind. There is often a childlike quality in the emotions of supernatural beings with which children can identify. Many good translations of myths exist for readers of varying abilities, but Edith Hamilton's *Mythology* is the most definitive reading for adolescents.

Fairy tales

Fairy tales are lively fictional stories involving children or animals that come in contact with super-beings via magic. They provide happy solutions to human dilemmas. The fairy tales of many nations are peopled by trolls, elves, dwarfs, and pixies, child-sized beings capable of fantastic accomplishments.

Among the most famous are "Beauty and the Beast," "Cinderella," "Hansel and Gretel," "Snow White and the Seven Dwarfs," "Rumplestiltskin," and "Tom Thumb." In each tale, the protagonist survives prejudice, imprisonment, ridicule, and even death to receive justice in a cruel world.

Older readers encounter a kind of fairy tale world in Shakespeare's *The Tempest* and *A Midsummer Night's Dream*, which use pixies and fairies as characters. Adolescent readers today are as fascinated by the creations of fantasy realms in the works of Piers Anthony, Ursula LeGuin, and Anne McCaffrey. An extension of interest in the supernatural is the popularity of science fiction that allows us to use current knowledge to predict the possible course of the future.

Angels (or sometimes fairy godmothers) play a role in some fairy tales, and Milton in Paradise Lost and Paradise Regained also used symbolic angels and devils.

Biblical stories provide many allusions. Parables, moralistic like fables but having human characters, include the stories of the Good Samaritan and the Prodigal Son. References to the treachery of Cain and the betrayal of Christ by Judas Iscariot are oft-cited examples.

American folk tales

American folktales are divided into two categories.

Imaginary tales, also called tall tales (humorous tales based on non-existent, fictional characters developed through blatant exaggeration)

> John Henry is a two-fisted steel driver who beats out a steam drill in competition.
>
> Rip Van Winkle sleeps for twenty years in the Catskill Mountains and upon awakening cannot understand why no one recognizes him.
>
> Paul Bunyan, a giant lumberjack, owns a great blue ox named Babe and has extraordinary physical strength. He is said to have plowed the Mississippi River while the impression of Babe's hoof prints created the Great Lakes.

Real tales, also called legends (based on real persons who accomplished the feats that are attributed to them even if they are slightly exaggerated)

> For more than forty years, Johnny Appleseed (John Chapman) roamed Ohio and Indiana planting apple seeds.
>
> Daniel Boone - scout, adventurer, and pioneer - blazed the Wilderness Trail and made Kentucky safe for settlers.
>
> Paul Revere, an colonial patriot, rode through the New England countryside warning of the approach of British troops.
>
> George Washington cut down a cherry tree, which he could not deny, or did he?

Skill 18.2 Analyze the expression of cultural values and ideas through literature.

Literature is powerful in influencing the thinking of individual readers and all of society. Waves of philosophical ideas have swept over the reading world almost from the time of the invention of the printing press. It's possible to trace the emergence of a particular set of values over centuries. Feminism is a case in point. While the matter of women's rights didn't reach a boiling point until the 1960s, it can be traced through history for many years.

For example, Empress Theodora of Byzantium was a proponent of legislation that would afford greater protections and freedoms to her female subjects, and Christine de Pizan, the first professional female writer, advanced many feminist ideas as early as the 1300s in the face of attempts to restrict female inheritance and guild membership. In 1869, John Stuart Mill published *The Subjection of Women* to demonstrate that "the legal subordination of one sex to the other is wrong…and…one of the chief hindrances to human improvement." Norwegian playwright Henrik Ibsen wrote the highly controversial play, *A Doll's House,* in 1879, a scathing criticism of the traditional roles of men and women in Victorian marriages. These and many other works with feminist themes led to changes in the way society viewed women throughout the civilized world. The impact of the literature and the changes in thinking on this issue led to many countries' granting of the vote to women in the late 1800s and the early years of the 20th century.

Regional literature has played an important role in the themes of popular literature, particularly in American literature. The best-known of the regional American writers is Samuel Langhorne Clemens, better known as Mark Twain with his stories about the Mississippi River and the state of Missouri. Although his home state was a slave state and considered by many to be part of the South, it declined to join the Confederacy and remained loyal to the union. He wrote sympathetic slave characters in many of his stories.

Some regional American writers:
Harriet Beecher Stowe
Sarah Orne Jewett
George Washington Cable
Joel Chandler Harris
Edward Eggleston
James Whitcomb Riley
Bret Harte

Ethnic themes are also very popular in American literature. Toni Morrison, who writes African-American stories, is considered to be the most important American writer of the last 25 years and won the Nobel Prize for Literature in 1993 for her collected works. Saul Bellow wrote of his own Jewish backgrounds and also won the Nobel Prize in 1976.

James Michener wrote history as fiction in his many novels: *Tales of the South Pacific* (for which he won the Pulitzer Prize for Fiction in 1948), *Hawaii*, *The Drifters*, *Centennial*, *The Source*, *The Fires of Spring*, *Chesapeake*, *Caribbean*, *Caravans*, *Alaska*, *Texas*, and *Poland*.

Literature about a particular period has also been very popular with American writers. The Civil War era has been a very successful subject for novelists, most notable of which is *Gone With the Wind* by Margaret Mitchell.

Some novels about the American Civil War:
- *The Red Badge of Courage* by Stephen Crane
- *Cold Mountain* by Charles Frazier
- *Love and War* by John Jakes
- *Gods and Generals*; *The Last Full Measure* by Jeffrey Shaara
- *By Valour and Arms* by James Street
- *Fort Pillow* by Harry Turtledove
- *Lincoln* by Gore Vidal

Skill 18.3 Analyze the role of given authors and works in influencing public opinion about and understanding of social issues.

Writers, from the time of the invention of the printing press, have played important roles in shaping public opinion, not only in their own countries but also around the world. Worldwide philosophical trends can be traced to the literature that was popular in a particular period of time. America has always been a nation of readers. With the development of theaters and ultimately movies and television that often dramatized popular novels, the power of the written word has increased.

John Steinbeck's *Grapes of Wrath* focused the attention of Americans on the plight of the common people who suffered more than anyone else because of the Great Depression. His revelation that Americans were starving to death in a land of great abundance still resonates with the public.

Members of the "establishment" in the farms and towns of California are revealed as callous and greedy. Church members, particularly clergy and leaders, don't come off much better in his revealing story. Steinbeck lived with some of the migrants so he could write authentically and with first-hand knowledge. Many of the writers who have influenced public opinion write from personal experience.

The feminist movement has virtually been fueled by literature going back several hundred years. Although the organized movement began with the first women's rights convention at Seneca Falls, New York, in 1948, in 1869, John Stuart Mill had already published *The Subjection of Women* to demonstrate that the legal subordination of one sex to the other is wrong. Virginia Woolf's essay, *A Room of One's Own*, first published in 1929, had a strong influence on how women were beginning to see their roles.

However, in the crusade that was ignited by the Civil Rights movement of the 1960s, Betty Friedan's book, *The Feminine Mystique*, published in 1963, was very popular and influenced many women to become involved, both in changes in their own outlooks and behaviors, but also in the movement at large as activists. Feminism has been so much a part of the thinking throughout the world that it should always be included in the potential themes one looks for when writing a critique of a literary work.

Uncle Tom's Cabin broke new ground in literature on social injustice and was very powerful in influencing the thinking of American people about slavery. It was the best-selling novel of the 19th century and is credited with helping to fuel the abolitionist cause prior to the American Civil War. Written by Harriet Beecher Stowe and published in 1852, slavery is its central theme.

The Vietnam War inspired many novels although most were written after the war was over. However, the attitudes of Americans about the war have been influenced by these novels, and for many, they have formed the concept they carry with them about the conflict.

Some examples of novels about the Vietnam War:
- *Apocalypse Now*
- *Full Metal Jacket*
- *Platoon*
- *Good Morning Vietnam*
- *The Deer Hunter*
- *Born on the Fourth of July*
- *Hamburger Hill*

COMPETENCY 19.0 UNDERSTAND CLASSIC AND CONTEMPORARY LITERATURE FOR YOUNG ADOLESCENTS

Skill 19.1 Demonstrate knowledge of characteristics of writers, works, and genres of literature for young adolescents.

Prior to twentieth century research on child development and child/adolescent literature's relationship to that development, books for adolescents were primarily didactic. They were designed to be instructive of history, manners, and morals.

Middle Ages

As early as the eleventh century, Anselm, the Archbishop of Canterbury, wrote an encyclopedia designed to instill in children the beliefs and principles of conduct acceptable to adults in medieval society. Early monastic translations of the *Bible* and other religious writings were written in Latin, for the edification of the upper class. Fifteenth century hornbooks were designed to teach reading and religious lessons. William Caxton printed English versions of *Aesop's Fables*, Malory's *Le Morte d'Arthur* and stories from Greek and Roman mythology. Though printed for adults, tales of adventures of Odysseus and the Arthurian knights were also popular with literate adolescents.

Renaissance

The Renaissance saw the introduction of the inexpensive chapbooks, small in size and 16-64 pages in length. Chapbooks were condensed versions of mythology and fairy tales. Designed for the common people, chapbooks were imperfect grammatically but were immensely popular because of their adventurous contents. Though most of the serious, educated adults frowned on the sometimes-vulgar little books, they received praise from Richard Steele of *Tatler* fame for inspiring his grandson's interest in reading and pursuing his other studies.

Meanwhile, the Puritans' three most popular reads were the *Bible*, John Foxe's *Book of Martyrs*, and John Bunyan's *Pilgrim's Progress*. Though venerating religious martyrs and preaching the moral propriety which was to lead to eternal happiness, the stories of the *Book of Martyrs* were often lurid in their descriptions of the fate of the damned. Not written for children and difficult reading even for adults, *Pilgrim's Progress* was as attractive to adolescents for its adventurous plot as for its moral outcome. In Puritan America, the *New England Primer* set forth the prayers, catechisms, *Bible* verses, and illustrations meant to instruct children in the Puritan ethic. The seventeenth-century French used fables and fairy tales to entertain adults, but children found them enjoyable as well.

Seventeenth century

The late seventeenth century brought the first concern with providing literature that specifically targeted the young.

Pierre Perrault's *Fairy Tales*, Jean de la Fontaine's retellings of famous fables, Mme. d'Aulnoy's novels based on old folktales, and Mme. de Beaumont's "Beauty and the Beast" were written to delight as well as instruct young people. In England, publisher John Newbury was the first to publish a line for children. These include a translation of Perrault's *Tales of Mother Goose; A Little Pretty Pocket-Book*, "intended for instruction and amusement" but decidedly moralistic and bland in comparison to the previous century's chapbooks; and *The Renowned History of Little Goody Two Shoes*, allegedly written by Oliver Goldsmith for a juvenile audience.

Eighteenth century

By and large, however, into the eighteenth century adolescents were finding their reading pleasure in adult books: Daniel Defoe's *Robinson Crusoe*, Jonathan Swift's *Gulliver's Travels*, and Johann Wyss's *Swiss Family Robinson*. More books were being written for children, but the moral didacticism, though less religious, was nevertheless ever present. The short stories of Maria Edgeworth, the four-volume *The History of Sandford and Merton* by Thomas Day, and Martha Farquharson's twenty-six volume *Elsie Dinsmore* series dealt with pious protagonists who learned restraint, repentance, and rehabilitation from sin. Two bright spots in this period of didacticism were Jean Jacques Rousseau's *Emile* and *The Tales of Shakespeare*, Charles and Mary Lamb's simplified versions of Shakespeare's plays. Rousseau believed that a child's abilities were enhanced by a free, happy life, and the Lambs subscribed to the notion that children were entitled to more entertaining literature in language comprehensible to them.

Nineteenth century

Child/adolescent literature truly began its modern rise in nineteenth century Europe. Hans Christian Andersen's *Fairy Tales* were fanciful adaptations of the somber revisions of the Grimm brothers in the previous century. Andrew Lang's series of colorful fairy books contain the folklores of many nations and are still part of the collections of many modern libraries. Clement Moore's "A Visit from St. Nicholas" is a cheery, non-threatening child's view of the "night before Christmas." The humor of Lewis Carroll's books about Alice's adventures, Edward Lear's poems with caricatures, Lucretia Nole's stories of the Philadelphia Peterkin family, were full of fancy and not a smidgen of morality. Other popular Victorian novels introduced the modern fantasy and science fiction genres: William Makepeace Thackeray's *The Rose and the Ring*, Charles Dickens' *The Magic Fishbone*, and Jules Verne's *Twenty Thousand Leagues Under the Sea*. Adventure to exotic places became a popular topic: Rudyard Kipling's *Jungle Books*, Verne's *Around the World in Eighty Days*, and Robert Louis Stevenson's *Treasure Island* and *Kidnapped*. In 1884, the first English translation Johanna Spyre's *Heidi* appeared.

North America was also finding its voices for adolescent readers. American Louisa May Alcott's *Little Women* and Canadian L.M. Montgomery's *Anne of Green Gables* ushered in the modern age of realistic fiction.

American youth were enjoying the articles of Tom Sawyer and Huckleberry Finn. For the first time children were able to read books about real people just like themselves.

Twentieth century

The literature of the twentieth century is extensive and diverse, and as in previous centuries much influenced by the adults who write, edit, and select books for youth consumption. In the first third of the century, suitable adolescent literature dealt with children from good homes with large families. These books projected an image of a peaceful, rural existence. Though the characters and plots were more realistic, the stories maintained focus on topics that were considered emotionally and intellectually proper. Popular at this time were Laura Ingalls Wilder's Little House on the Prairie Series and Carl Sandburg's biography *Abe Lincoln Grows Up*. English author J.R.R. Tolkein's fantasy *The Hobbit* prefaced modern adolescent readers' fascination with the works of Piers Antony, Madelaine L'Engle, and Anne McCaffery.

Skill 19.2   Analyze in passage context major thematic elements associated with adolescent literature.

Adolescent literature, because of the age range of readers, is extremely diverse. Fiction for the middle group, usually ages ten/eleven to fourteen/fifteen, deals with issues of coping with internal and external changes in their lives. Because children's writers in the twentieth century have produced increasingly realistic fiction, adolescents can now find problems dealt with honestly in novels.

Teachers of middle/junior high school students see the greatest change in interests and reading abilities. Fifth and sixth graders, included in elementary grades in many schools, are viewed as older children while seventh and eighth graders are preadolescent. Ninth graders, included sometimes as top dogs in junior high school and sometimes as underlings in high school, definitely view themselves as teenagers. Their literature choices will often be governed more by interest than by ability; thus, the wealth of high-interest, low readability books that have flooded the market in recent years. Tenth through twelfth graders will still select high-interest books for pleasure reading but are also easily encouraged to stretch their literature muscles by reading more classics.

Because of the rapid social changes, topics that once did not interest young people until they reached their teens - suicide, gangs, homosexuality - are now subjects of books for even younger readers. The plethora of high-interest books reveals how desperately schools have failed to produce on-level readers and how the market has adapted to that need. However, these high-interest books are now readable for younger children whose reading levels are at or above normal. No matter how tastefully written, some contents are inappropriate for younger readers.

The problem becomes not so much steering them toward books that they have the reading ability to handle but encouraging them toward books whose content is appropriate to their levels of cognitive and social development. A fifth-grader may be able to read V.C. Andrews book *Flowers in the Attic* but not possess the social/moral development to handle the deviant behavior of the characters. At the same time, because of the complex changes affecting adolescents, the teacher must be well versed in learning theory and child development as well as competent to teach the subject matter of language and literature.

Skill 19.3   Examine ways in which adolescent readers gain insights into themselves and others through literature.

Reading literature involves a reciprocal interaction between the reader and the text.

Types of responses

Emotional

The reader can identify with the characters and situations so as to project himself into the story. The reader feels a sense of satisfaction by associating aspects of his own life with the people, places, and events in the literature. Emotional responses are observed in a reader's verbal and non-verbal reactions - laughter, comments on its effects, and retelling or dramatizing the action.

Interpretive

Interpretive responses result in inferences about character development, setting, or plot; analysis of style elements - metaphor, simile, allusion, rhythm, tone; outcomes derivable from information provided in the narrative; and assessment of the author's intent. Interpretive responses are made verbally or in writing.

Critical

Critical responses involve making value judgments about the quality of a piece of literature. Reactions to the effectiveness of the writer's style and language use are observed through discussion and written reactions.

Evaluative

Some reading response theory researchers also add a response that considers the readers considerations of such factors as how well the piece of literature represents its genre, how well it reflects the social/ethical mores of society, and how well the author has approached the subject for freshness and slant.

Middle school readers will exhibit both emotional and interpretive responses. Naturally, making interpretive responses depends on the degree of knowledge the student has of literary elements. A child's being able to say why a particular book was boring or why a particular poem made him sad evidences critical reactions on a fundamental level. Adolescents in ninth and tenth grades should begin to make critical responses by addressing the specific language and genre characteristics of literature. Evaluative responses are harder to detect and are rarely made by any but a few advanced high school students. However, if the teacher knows what to listen for, she can recognize evaluative responses and incorporate them into discussions.

For example, if a student says, "I don't understand why that character is doing that," he is making an interpretive response to character motivation. However, if he goes on to say, "What good is that action?" he is giving an evaluative response that should be explored in terms of "What good should it do and why isn't that positive action happening?"

At the emotional level, the student says, "I almost broke into a sweat when he was describing the heat in the burning house." An interpretive response says, "The author used descriptive adjectives to bring his setting to life." Critically, the student adds, "The author's use of descriptive language contributes to the success of the narrative and maintains reader interest through the whole story." If he goes on to wonder why the author allowed the grandmother in the story to die in the fire, he is making an evaluative response.

Levels of response

The levels of reader response will depend largely on the reader's level of social, psychological, and intellectual development. Most middle school students have progressed beyond merely involving themselves in the story enough to be able to retell the events in some logical sequence or describe the feeling that the story evoked. They are aware to some degree that the feeling evoked was the result of a careful manipulation of good elements of fiction writing. They may not explain that awareness as successfully as a high school student, but they are beginning to grasp the concepts and not just the personal reactions. They are beginning to differentiate between responding to the story itself and responding to a literary creation.

Fostering self-esteem and empathy for others and the world in which one lives

All-important is the use of literature as bibliotherapy that allows the reader to identify with others and become aware of alternatives, yet not feeling directly betrayed or threatened. For the high school student the ability to empathize is an evaluative response, a much desired outcome of literature studies. Use of these books either individually or as a thematic unit of study allows for discussion or writing. The titles are grouped by theme, not by reading level.

ABUSE:

Blair, Maury and Brendel, Doug. *Maury, Wednesday's Child*

Dizenzo, Patricia. *Why Me?*

Parrot, Andrea. *Coping with Date Rape and Acquaintance Rape*

NATURAL WORLD CONCERNS:

Caduto, M. and Bruchac, J. *Keeper's of Earth*

Gay, Kathlyn. *Greenhouse Effect*

Johnson, Daenis. *Fiskadaro*

Madison, Arnold. *It Can't Happen to Me*

EATING DISORDERS:

Arnold, Caroline. *Too Fat, Too Thin, Do I Have a Choice?*

DeClements, Barthe. *Nothing's Fair in Fifth Grade*

Snyder, Anne. *Goodbye, Paper Doll*

FAMILY

Chopin, Kate. *The Runner*

Cormier, Robert. *Tunes for Bears to Dance to*

Danzinger, Paula. *The Divorce Express*

Neufield, John. *Sunday Father*

Okimoto, Jean Davies. *Molly by any Other Name*

Peck, Richard. *Don't Look and It Won't Hurt*

Zindel, Paul. *I Never Loved Your Mind*

STEREOTYPING:

Baklanov, Grigory. (Trans. by Antonina W. Bouis) *Forever Nineteen*

Kerr, M.E. *Gentle Hands*

Greene, Betty. *Summer of My German Soldier*

Reiss, Johanna. *The Upstairs Room*

Taylor, Mildred D. *Roll of Thunder, Hear Me Cry*

Wakatsuki-Houston, Jeanne and Houston, James D. *Farewell to Manzanar*

SUICIDE AND DEATH:

Blume, Judy. *Tiger Eyes*

Bunting, Eve. *If I Asked You, Would You Stay?*

Gunther, John. *Death Be Not Proud*

Mazer, Harry. *When the Phone Rings*

Peck, Richard. *Remembering the Good Times*

Richter, Elizabeth. *Losing Someone You Love*

Strasser, Todd. *Friends Till the End*

Cautions

There is always a caution when reading materials of a sensitive or controversial nature. The teacher must be cognizant of the happenings in the school and outside community to spare students undue suffering. A child who has known a recent death in his family or circle of friends may need to distance himself from classroom discussion. Whenever open discussion of a topic brings pain or embarrassment, the child should not be further subjected. Older children and young adults will be able to discuss issues with greater objectivity and without making blurted, insensitive comments. The teacher must be able to gauge the level of emotional development of her students when selecting subject matter and the strategies for studying it. The student or his parents may consider some material objectionable. Should a student choose not to read an assigned material, it is the teacher's responsibility to allow the student to select an alternate title. It is always advisable to notify parents if a particularly sensitive piece is to be studied.

Skill 19.4   Identify criteria for selecting literature for young adolescents.

These classic and contemporary works combine the characteristics of multiple theories. Functioning at the concrete operations stage (Piaget), being of the "good person," orientation (Kohlberg), still highly dependent on external rewards (Bandura), and exhibiting all five needs previously discussed from Maslow's hierarchy, these eleven to twelve year olds should appreciate the following titles, grouped by reading level. These titles are also cited for interest at that grade level and do not reflect high-interest titles for older readers who do not read at grade level. Some high interest titles will be cited later.

Reading level 6.0 to 6.9

Barrett, William. *Lilies of the Field*
Cormier, Robert. *Other Bells for Us to Ring*
Dahl, Roald. *Danny, Champion of the World; Charlie and the Chocolate Factory*
Lindgren, Astrid. *Pippi Longstocking*
Lindbergh, Anne. *Three Lives to Live*
Lowry, Lois. *Rabble Starkey*
Naylor, Phyllis. *The Year of the Gopher, Reluctantly Alice*
Peck, Robert Newton. *Arly*
Speare, Elizabeth. *The Witch of Blackbird Pond*
Sleator, William. *The Boy Who Reversed Himself*

For seventh and eighth grades

Most seventh and eight grade students, according to learning theory, are still functioning cognitively, psychologically, and morally as sixth graders. As these are not inflexible standards, there are some twelve and thirteen year olds who are much more mature socially, intellectually, and physically than the younger children who share the same school. They are becoming concerned with establishing individual and peer group identities that presents conflicts with breaking from authority and the rigidity of rules. Some at this age are still tied firmly to the family and its expectations while others identify more with those their own age or older. Enrichment reading for this group must help them cope with life's rapid changes or provide escape and thus must be either realistic or fantastic depending on the child's needs. Adventures and mysteries (the Hardy Boys and Nancy Drew series) are still popular today. These preteens also become more interested in biographies of contemporary figures rather than legendary figures of the past.

Reading level 7.0 to 7.9

Armstrong, William. *Sounder*
Bagnold, Enid. *National Velvet*
Barrie, James. *Peter Pan*
London, Jack. *White Fang, Call of the Wild*
Lowry, Lois. *Taking Care of Terrific*
McCaffrey, Anne. The *Dragonsinger* series
Montgomery, L. M. *Anne of Green Gables* and sequels
Steinbeck, John. *The Pearl*
Tolkien, J. R. R. *The Hobbit*
Zindel, Paul. *The Pigman*

Reading level 8.0 to 8.9

    Cormier, Robert. *I Am the Cheese*
    McCullers, Carson. *The Member of the Wedding*
    North, Sterling. *Rascal*
    Twain, Mark. *The Adventures of Tom Sawyer*
    Zindel, Paul. *My Darling , My Hamburger*

For ninth grade

Depending upon the school environment, a ninth grader may be top-dog in a junior high school or underdog in a high school. Much of his social development and thus his reading interests become motivated by his peer associations. He is technically an adolescent operating at the early stages of formal operations in cognitive development. His perception of his own identity is becoming well-defined and he is fully aware of the ethics required by society. He is more receptive to the challenges of classic literature but still enjoys popular teen novels.

Reading level 9.0 to 9.9

    Brown, Dee. *Bury My Heart at Wounded Knee*
    Defoe, Daniel. *Robinson Crusoe*
    Dickens, Charles. *David Copperfield*
    Greenberg, Joanne. *I Never Promised You a Rose Garden*
    Kipling, Rudyard. *Captains Courageous*
    Mathabane, Mark. *Kaffir Boy*
    Nordhoff, Charles. *Mutiny on the Bounty*
    Shelley, Mary. *Frankenstein*
    Washington, Booker T. *Up From Slavery*

COMPETENCY 20.0 UNDERSTAND MAJOR THEMES, CHARACTERISTICS, TRENDS, WRITERS, AND WORKS IN AMERICAN, BRITISH, AND WORLD LITERATURE

Skill 20.1 Examine the role of major writers, works, and movements in the development of American, British, and world literature.

American Literature

The Colonial Period

William Bradford's excerpts from *The Mayflower Compact* relate vividly the hardships of crossing the Atlantic in such a tiny vessel, the misery and suffering of the first winter, the approaches of the American Indians, the decimation of their ranks, and the establishment of the Bay Colony of Massachusetts.

Anne Bradstreet's poetry relates much concerning colonial New England life. From her journals, modern readers learn of the everyday life of the early settlers, the hardships of travel, and the responsibilities of different groups and individuals in the community, Early American literature also reveals the commercial and political adventures of the Cavaliers who came to the New World with King George's blessing.

William Byrd's journal, *A History of the Dividing Line,* concerning his trek into the Dismal Swamp separating the Carolinian territories from Virginia and Maryland makes quite lively reading. A privileged insider to the English Royal Court, Byrd, like other Southern Cavaliers, was given grants to pursue business ventures.

The Revolutionary Period

There were great orations such as Patrick Henry's *Speech to the Virginia House of Burgesses* -- the "Give me liberty or give me death" speech - and George Washington's *Farewell to the Army of the Potomac.* Less memorable and thought rambling by modern readers are Washington's inaugural addresses.

The *Declaration of Independence*, the brainchild predominantly of Thomas Jefferson, with some prudent editing by Ben Franklin, is a prime example of neoclassical writing -- balanced, well crafted, and focused.

Epistles include the exquisitely written, moving correspondence between John Adams and Abigail Adams. The poignancy of their separation - she in Boston, he in Philadelphia - is palpable and real.

The Romantic Period

Nathaniel Hawthorne and Herman Melville are the preeminent early American novelists, writing on subjects definitely regional, specific and American, yet sharing insights about human foibles, fears, loves, doubts, and triumphs.

Hawthorne's writings range from children's stories, like the Cricket on the Hearth series, to adult fare of dark, brooding short stories such as "Dr. Heidegger's Experiment," "The Devil and Tom Walker," and "Rapuccini's Daughter." His masterpiece, *The Scarlet Letter*, takes on the society of hypocritical Puritan New Englanders, who ostensibly left England to establish religious freedom, but who have been entrenched in judgmental finger wagging. They ostracize Hester and condemn her child, Pearl, as a child of Satan. Great love, sacrifice, loyalty, suffering, and related epiphanies add universality to this tale. *The House of the Seven Gables* also deals with kept secrets, loneliness, societal pariahs, and love ultimately triumphing over horrible wrong. Herman Melville's great opus, *Moby Dick*, follows a crazed Captain Ahab on his Homeric odyssey to conquer the great white whale that has outwitted him and his whaling crews time and again. The whale has even taken Arab's leg and according to Ahab, wants all of him. Melville recreates in painstaking detail, and with insider knowledge of the harsh life of a whaler out of New Bedford, by way of Nantucket. For those who don't want to learn about every guy rope or all parts of the whaler's rigging, Melville offers up the succinct tale of Billy Budd and his Christ-like sacrifice to the black and white maritime laws on the high seas. An accident results in the death of one of the ship's officers, a slug of a fellow, who had taken a dislike to the young, affable, shy Billy. Captain Vere must hang Billy for the death of Claggert, but knows that this is not right. However, an example must be given to the rest of the crew so that discipline can be maintained.

Edgar Allan Poe creates a distinctly American version of romanticism with his 16 syllable line in "The Raven," the classical "To Helen," and his Gothic "Annabelle Lee." The horror short story can be said to originate from Poe's pen. "The Tell-Tale Heart," "The Cask of Amontillado," "The Fall of the House of Usher," and "The Masque of the Red Death" are exemplary short stories. The new genre of detective story also emerges with Poe's "Murders in the Rue Morgue."

American Romanticism has its own offshoot in the Transcendentalism of Ralph Waldo Emerson and Henry David Thoreau. One wrote about transcending the complexities of life; the other, who wanted to get to the marrow of life, pitted himself against nature at Walden Pond and wrote an inspiring autobiographical account of his sojourn, aptly titled *On Walden Pond*. He also wrote passionately on his objections to the interference of government on the individual in "On the Duty of Civil Disobedience."

Emerson's elegantly crafted essays and war poetry still give validation to several important universal truths. Probably most remembered for his address to Thoreau's Harvard graduating class, "The American Scholar," he defined the qualities of hard work and intellectual spirit required of Americans in their growing nation.

The Transition between Romanticism and Realism

The Civil War period ushers in the poignant poetry of Walt Whitman and his homages to all who suffer from the ripple effects of war and presidential assassination. His "Come up from the Fields, Father" about a Civil War soldier's death and his family's reaction and "When Lilacs Last in the Courtyard Bloom'd" about the effects of Abraham Lincoln's death on the poet and the nation should be required readings in any American literature course. Further, his *Leaves of Grass* gave America its first poetry truly unique in form, structure, and subject matter.

Emily Dickinson, like Walt Whitman, leaves her literary fingerprints on a vast array of poems, all but three of which were never published in her lifetime. Her themes of introspection and attention to nature's details and wonders are, by any measurement, world-class works. Her posthumous recognition reveals the timeliness of her work. American writing had most certainly arrived!

Mark Twain also left giant footprints with his unique blend of tall tale and fable. "The Celebrated Jumping Frog of Calaveras County" and "The Man who Stole Hadleyburg" are epitomes of short story writing. Move to novel creation, and Twain again rises head and shoulders above others by his bold, still disputed, oft-banned *The Adventures of Huckleberry Finn*, which examines such taboo subjects as a white person's love of a slave, the issue of leaving children with abusive parents, and the outcomes of family feuds. Written partly in dialect and southern vernacular, *The Adventures of Huckleberry Finn* is touted by some as the greatest American novel.

Contemporary American Literature

America Drama

The greatest and most prolific of American playwrights include:

Eugene O'Neill -- *Long Day's Journey into Night, Mourning Becomes Electra,* and *Desire Under the Elms*

Arthur Miller -- *The Crucible, All My Sons,* and *Death of a Salesman*

Tennessee Williams -- *Cat on a Hot Tin Roof, The Glass Menagerie,* and *A Street Car Named Desire*

Edward Albee -- *Who's Afraid of Virginia Woolf?, Three Tall Women,* and *A Delicate Balance*

American Fiction

The renowned American novelists of this century include

John Updike -- *Rabbit Run* and *Rabbit Redux*

Sinclair Lewis -- *Babbit* and *Elmer Gantry*

F. Scott Fitzgerald -- *The Great Gatsby* and *Tender is the Night*

Ernest Hemingway -- *A Farewell to Arms* and *For Whom the Bell Tolls*

William Faulkner -- *The Sound and the Fury* and *Absalom, Absalom*

Bernard Malamud -- *The Fixer* and *The Natural*

American Poetry

The poetry of the twentieth century is multifaceted, as represented by Edna St. Vincent Millay, Marianne Moore, Richard Wilbur, Langston Hughes, Maya Angelou, and Rita Lone. Head and shoulders above all others are the many-layered poems of Robert Frost. His New England motifs of snowy evenings, birches, apple picking, stone wall mending, hired hands, and detailed nature studies relate universal truths in exquisite diction, polysyllabic words, and rare allusions to either mythology or the *Bible*.

American Literature is defined by a number of clearly identifiable periods.

1. Native American works from various tribes

These were originally part of a vast oral tradition that spanned most of continental America from as far back as before the 15th century.

- Characteristics of native Indian literature include
  - Reverence for and awe of nature.
  - The interconnectedness of the elements in the life cycle.

- Themes of Indian literature often reflect
  - The hardiness of the native body and soul.
  - Remorse for the destruction of their way of life.
  - The genocide of many tribes by the encroaching settlement and Manifest Destiny policies of the U. S. government.

2. The Colonial Period in both New England and the South

Stylistically, early colonists' writings were neo-classical, emphasizing order, balance, clarity, and reason. Schooled in England, their writing and speaking was still decidedly British even as their thinking became entirely American.

Early American literature reveals the lives and experiences of the New England expatriates who left England to find religious freedom.

The Revolutionary Period contains non-fiction genres: essay, pamphlet, speech, famous document, and epistle.

Thomas Paine's pamphlet, *Common Sense*, which, though written by a recently transplanted Englishman, spoke to the American patriots' common sense in dealing with the issues in the cause of freedom.

Other contributions are Benjamin Franklin's essays from *Poor Richard's Almanac* and satires such as "How to Reduce a Great Empire to a Small One" and "A Letter to Madame Gout."

3. **The Romantic Period**

Early American folktales, and the emergence of a distinctly American writing, not just a stepchild to English forms, constitute the next period.

Washington Irving's characters, Icabod Crane and Rip Van Winkle, create a uniquely American folklore devoid of English influences. The characters are indelibly marked by their environment and the superstitions of the New Englander. The early American writings of James Fenimore Cooper and his Leatherstocking Tales with their stirring accounts of drums along the Mohawk and the French and Indian Wars, the futile British defense of Fort William Henry and the brutalities of this time frame allow readers a window into their uniquely American world. Natty Bumppo, Chingachgook, Uncas, and Magua are unforgettable characters that reflect the American spirit in thought and action.

The poetry of Fireside Poets - James Russell Lowell, Oliver Wendell Holmes, Henry Wadsworth Longfellow, and John Greenleaf Whittier - was recited by American families and read in the long New England winters. In "The Courtin'," Lowell used Yankee dialect to tell a narrative. Spellbinding epics by Longfellow such as *Hiawatha*, *The Courtship of Miles Standish*, and *Evangeline* told of adversity, sorrow, and ultimate happiness in an uniquely American warp. "Snowbound" by Whittier relates the story of a captive family isolated by a blizzard, stressing family closeness. Holmes' "The Chambered Nautilus" and his famous line, "Fired the shot heard round the world," put American poetry on a firm footing with other world writers.

4. **The Transition between Romanticism and Realism**

During this period such legendary figures as Paul Bunyan and Pecos Bill rose from the oral tradition. Anonymous storytellers around campfires told tales of a huge lumberman and his giant blue ox, Babe, whose adventures were explanations of natural phenomena like those of footprints filled with rainwater becoming the Great Lakes.

Or the whirling-dervish speed of Pecos Bill explained the tornadoes of the Southwest. Like ancient peoples, finding reasons for the happenings in their lives, these American pioneer storytellers created a mythology appropriate to the vast reaches of the unsettled frontier.

5. **The Realistic Period**

The late nineteenth century saw a reaction against the tendency of romantic writers to look at the world through rose-colored glasses. Writers like Frank Norris (*The Pit*) and Upton Sinclair (*The Jungle*) used their novels to decry conditions for workers in slaughterhouses and wheat mills. In *The Red Badge of Courage*, Stephen Crane wrote of the daily sufferings of the common soldier in the Civil War. Realistic writers wrote of common, ordinary people and events using detail that would reveal the harsh realities of life. They broached taboos by creating protagonists whose environments often destroyed them. Romantic writers would have only protagonists whose indomitable wills helped them rise above adversity. Crane's *Maggie: A Girl of the Streets* deals with a young woman forced into prostitution to survive. In "The Occurrence at Owl Creek Bridge," Ambrose Bierce relates the unfortunate hanging of a Confederate soldier.

Upton Sinclair

Short stories, like Bret Harte's "The Outcasts of Poker Flat" and Jack London's "To Build a Fire," deal with unfortunate people whose luck in life has run out. Many writers, sub-classified as naturalists, believed that man was subject to a fate over which he had no control.

6. **The Modern Era**

The twentieth century American writing can be classified into three basic genres:

- Drama
- Fiction
- Poetry

British Literature

There are four major time periods of writings in British literature. They are neoclassicism, romanticism, realism, and naturalism. Certain authors, among these Chaucer, Shakespeare, and Donne, though writing during a particular literary period, are considered to have a style all their own.

Neoclassicism: Patterned after the greatest writings of classical Greece and Rome, this type of writing is characterized by balanced, graceful, well-crafted, refined, elevated style. Major proponents of this style are poet laureates, John Dryden and Alexander Pope. The eras in which they wrote are called the Ages of Dryden and Pope. The self is not exalted and focus is on the group, not the individual, in neoclassic writing.

Romanticism: Writings emphasizing the individual. Emotions and feelings are validated. Nature acts as an inspiration for creativity; it is a balm of the spirit. Romantics hearken back to medieval, chivalric themes and ambiance. They also emphasize supernatural, Gothic themes and settings, which are characterized by gloom and darkness. Imagination is stressed. New types of writings include detective and horror stories and autobiographical introspection (Wordsworth). There are two generations in British Literature: First Generation includes William Wordsworth and Samuel Taylor Coleridge whose collaboration, *Lyrical Ballads*, defines romanticism and its exponents. Wordsworth maintained that the scenes and events of everyday life and the speech of ordinary people were the raw material of which poetry could and should be made. Romanticism spread to the United States, where Ralph Waldo Emerson and Henry David Thoreau adopted it in their transcendental romanticism, emphasizing reasoning. Further extensions of this style are found in Edgar Allan Poe's Gothic writings. Second Generation romantics include the ill-fated Englishmen Lord Byron, John Keats, and Percy Bysshe Shelley. Byron and Shelley, who for some most epitomize the romantic poet (in their personal lives as well as in their work), wrote resoundingly in protest against social and political wrongs and in defense of the struggles for liberty in Italy and Greece. The Second Generation romantics stressed personal introspection and the love of beauty and nature as requisites of inspiration.

Realism: Unlike classical and neoclassical writing which, often deal with aristocracies and nobility or the gods, realistic writers deal with the common man and his socio/economic problems in a non-sentimental way. Muckraking, social injustice, domestic abuse, and inner city conflicts are examples of writings by writers of realism.

Realistic writers include Thomas Hardy, George Bernard Shaw, and Henrik Ibsen.

Naturalism: This is realism pushed to the maximum, writing which exposes the underbelly of society, usually the lower class struggles. This is the world of penury, injustice, abuse, ghetto survival, hungry children, single parenting, and substance abuse. Émile Zola was inspired by his readings in history and medicine and attempted to apply methods of scientific observation to the depiction of pathological human character, notably in his series of novels devoted to several generations of one French family.

Anglo-Saxon

The Anglo-Saxon period spans six centuries but produced only a smattering of literature. The first British epic is *Beowulf,* anonymously written by Christian monks many years after the events in the narrative supposedly occurred. This Teutonic saga relates the triumph three times over monsters by the hero, Beowulf. "The Seafarer," a shorter poem, some history, and some riddles are the rest of the Anglo-Saxon canon.

Medieval

The Medieval period introduces Geoffrey Chaucer, the father of English literature, whose *Canterbury Tales* are written in the vernacular, or street language of England, not in Latin. Thus, the tales are said to be the first work of British literature. Next, Thomas Malory's *Le Morte d'Arthur* calls together the extant tales from Europe as well as England concerning the legendary King Arthur, Merlin, Guenevere, and the Knights of the Round Table. This work is the generative work that gave rise to the many Arthurian legends that stir the chivalric imagination.

Renaissance and Elizabethan

The Renaissance, the most important period since it is synonymous with William Shakespeare, begins with importing the idea of the Petrarchan or Italian sonnet into England. Sir Thomas Wyatt and Sir Philip Sydney wrote English versions. Next, Sir Edmund Spenser invented a variation on this Italian sonnet form, aptly called the Spenserian sonnet. His masterpiece is the epic, *The Fairie Queene*, honoring Queen Elizabeth I's reign. He also wrote books on the Red Cross Knight, St. George and the Dragon, and a series of Arthurian adventures. Spencer was dubbed the Poet's Poet. He created a nine-line stanza, eight lines iambic pentameter and an extra-footed ninth line, an alexandrine. Thus, he invented the Spencerian stanza as well.

William Shakespeare, the Bard of Avon, wrote 154 sonnets, 39 plays, and two long narrative poems. The sonnets are justifiably called the greatest sonnet sequence in all literature.

Shakespeare dispensed with the octave/sestet format of the Italian sonnet and invented his three quatrains, one heroic couplet format. His plays are divided into comedies, history plays, and tragedies. Great lines from these plays are more often quoted than from any other author. The Big Four tragedies, Hamlet, *Macbeth*, *Othello*, and *King Lear* are acknowledged to be the most brilliant examples of this genre.

Analyzing passages that illustrate significant themes and characteristics of major British and Irish literary works of the Enlightenment, the romantic and Victorian periods, and the twentieth century (the satires of Swift, the odes of Keats, the fiction of Woolf, the drama of Beckett).

Seventeenth century

John Milton's devout Puritanism was the wellspring of his creative genius that closes the remarkable productivity of the English Renaissance. His social commentary in such works as *Aereopagitica*, *Samson Agonistes*, and his elegant sonnets would be enough to solidify his stature as a great writer. It is his masterpiece based in part on the Book of Genesis that places Milton very near the top of the rung of a handful of the most renowned of all writers. *Paradise Lost*, written in balanced, elegant Neoclassic form, truly does justify the ways of God to man. The greatest allegory about man's journey to the Celestial City (Heaven) was written at the end of the English Renaissance, as was John Bunyan's *The Pilgrim's Progress*, which describes virtues and vices personified. This work is, or was for a long time, second only to the *Bible* in numbers of copies printed and sold.

The Jacobean Age gave us the marvelously witty and cleverly constructed conceits of John Donne's metaphysical sonnets, as well as his insightful meditations, and his version of sermons or homilies. "Ask not for whom the bell tolls", and "No man is an island unto himself" are famous epigrams from Donne's *Meditations*. His most famous conceit is that which compares lovers to a footed compass traveling seemingly separate, but always leaning towards one another and conjoined in "A Valediction Forbidding Mourning."

Eighteenth century

Ben Johnson, author of the wickedly droll play, *Volpone,* and the Cavalier *carpe diem* poets Robert Herrick, Sir John Suckling, and Richard Lovelace also wrote during King James I's reign.

The Restoration and Enlightenment reflect the political turmoil of the regicide of Charles I, the Interregnum Puritan government of Oliver Cromwell, and the restoring of the monarchy to England by the coronation of Charles II, who had been given refuge by the French King Louis. Neoclassicism became the preferred writing style, especially for Alexander Pope.

New genres, such as *The Diary of Samuel Pepys*, the novels of Daniel Defoe, the periodical essays and editorials of Joseph Addison and Richard Steele, and Alexander Pope's mock epic, *The Rape of the Lock*, demonstrate the diversity of expression during this time.

Writers who followed were contemporaries of Dr. Samuel Johnson, the lexicographer of *The Dictionary of the English Language*. Fittingly, this Age of Johnson, which encompasses James Boswell's biography of Dr. Johnson, Robert Burns' Scottish dialect and regionalism in his evocative poetry and the mystical pre-Romantic poetry of William Blake usher in the Romantic Age and its revolution against Neoclassicism.

Romantic period

The Romantic Age encompasses what is known as the First Generation Romantics, William Wordsworth and Samuel Taylor Coleridge, who collaborated on *Lyrical Ballads,* which defines and exemplifies the tenets of this style of writing. The Second Generation includes George Gordon, Lord Byron, Percy Bysshe Shelley, and John Keats. These poets wrote sonnets, odes, epics, and narrative poems, most dealing with homage to nature. Wordsworth's most famous other works are "Intimations on Immortality" and "The Prelude." Byron's satirical epic, *Don Juan*, and his autobiographical *Childe Harold's Pilgrimage* are irreverent, witty, self-deprecating and, in part, cuttingly critical of other writers and critics. Shelley's odes and sonnets are remarkable for sensory imagery. Keats' sonnets, odes, and longer narrative poem, *The Eve of St. Agnes*, are remarkable for their introspection and the tender age of the poet, who died when he was only twenty-five. In fact, all of the Second Generation died before their times. Wordsworth, who lived to be eighty, outlived them all, as well as his friend and collaborator, Coleridge. Others who wrote during the Romantic Age are the essayist, Charles Lamb, and the novelist, Jane Austin. The Bronte sisters, Charlotte and Emily, wrote one novel each, which are noted as two of the finest ever written, *Jane Eyre* and *Wuthering Heights*. Marianne Evans, also known as George Eliot, wrote several important novels: her masterpiece, *Middlemarch*, *Silas Marner*, *Adam Bede*, and *Mill on the Floss*.

Nineteenth century

The Victorian Period is remarkable for the diversity and proliferation of work in three major areas. Poets who are typified as Victorians include Alfred, Lord Tennyson, who wrote *Idylls of the King*, twelve narrative poems about the Arthurian legend, and Robert Browning, who wrote chilling, dramatic monologues, such as "My Last Duchess," as well as long poetic narratives such as *The Pied Piper of Hamlin*. His wife Elizabeth wrote two major works, the epic feminist poem, *Aurora Leigh*, and her deeply moving and provocative *Sonnets from the Portuguese,* in which she details her deep love for Robert and his startling, to her, reciprocation. Gerard Manley Hopkins, a Catholic priest, wrote poetry with sprung rhythm. (See Glossary of Literary Terms in 2.2).

A. E. Housman, Matthew Arnold, and the Pre-Raphaelites, especially the brother and sister duo, Dante Gabriel Rosetti and Christina Rosetti, contributed much to round out the Victorian Era poetic scene. The Pre-Raphaelites, a group of 19th-century English painters, poets, and critics, reacted against Victorian materialism and the neoclassical conventions of academic art by producing earnest, quasi-religious works. Medieval and early Renaissance painters up to the time of the Italian painter Raphael inspired the group. Robert Louis Stevenson, the great Scottish novelist, wrote his adventure/history lessons for young adults. Victorian prose ranges from the incomparable, keenly woven plot structures of Charles Dickens to the deeply moving Dorset/Wessex novels of Thomas Hardy, in which women are repressed and life is more struggle than euphoria. Rudyard Kipling wrote about Colonialism in India in works like *Kim* and *The Jungle Book,* that create exotic locales and a distinct main point concerning the Raj, the British Colonial government during Queen Victoria's reign. Victorian drama is a product mainly of Oscar Wilde, whose satirical masterpiece, *The Importance of Being Earnest*, farcically details and lampoons Victorian social mores.

Twentieth century

The early twentieth century is represented mainly by the towering achievement of George Bernard Shaw's dramas: *St. Joan*, *Man and Superman*, *Major Barbara*, and *Arms and the Man,* to name a few. Novelists are too numerous to list, but Joseph Conrad, E. M. Forster, Virginia Woolf, James Joyce, Nadine Gordimer, Graham Greene, George Orwell, and D. H. Lawrence comprise some of the century's very best.

Twentieth century poets of renown and merit include W. H. Auden, Robert Graves, T. S. Eliot, Edith Sitwell, Stephen Spender, Dylan Thomas, Philip Larkin, Ted Hughes, Sylvia Plath, and Hugh MacDarmid. This list is by no means complete.

World Literature

Germany

German poet and playwright, Friedrich von Schiller, is best known for his history plays, *William Tell* and *The Maid of Orleans*. He is a leading literary figure in Germany's Golden Age of Literature. Also from Germany, Rainer Maria Rilke, the great lyric poet, is one of the poets of the unconscious, or stream of consciousness. Germany also has given the world Herman Hesse, (*Siddartha*), Gunter Grass (*The Tin Drum*), and the greatest of all German writers, Goethe.

Scandinavia

Scandinavia has encouraged the work of Hans Christian Andersen in Denmark, who advanced the fairy tale genre with such wistful tales as "The Little Mermaid" and "Thumbelina."

The social commentary of Henrik Ibsen in Norway startled the world of drama with such issues as feminism (*The Doll's House* and *Hedda Gabler*) and the effects of sexually transmitted diseases (*The Wild Duck* and *Ghosts*). Sweden's Selma Lagerlof is the first woman to ever win the Nobel Prize for literature. Her novels include *Gosta Berling's Saga* and the world-renowned *The Wonderful Adventures of Nils*, a children's work.

Russia

Russian literature is vast and monumental. Who has not heard of Fyodor Dostoyevski's *Crime and Punishment*, or *The Brothers Karamazov*, or Count Leo Tolstoy's *War and Peace*? These are examples of psychological realism. Dostoyevski's influence on modern writers cannot be overly stressed. Tolstoy's *War and Peace* is the sweeping account of the invasion of Russia and Napoleon's taking of Moscow, abandoned by the Russians. This novel is called the national novel of Russia. Further advancing Tolstoy's greatness is his ability to create believable, unforgettable female characters, especially Natasha in *War and Peace* and the heroine of *Anna Karenina*. Pushkin is famous for great short stories; Anton Chekhov for drama, (*Uncle Vanya*, *The Three Sisters*, *The Cherry Orchard*); Yvteshenko for poetry (*Babi Yar*).

France

France has a multifaceted canon of great literature that is universal in scope, almost always championing some social cause: the poignant short stories of Guy de Maupassant; the fantastic poetry of Charles Baudelaire (*Fleurs du Mal*); and the groundbreaking lyrical poetry of Rimbaud and Verlaine. Drama in France is best represented by Rostand's *Cyrano de Bergerac*, and the neo-classical dramas of Racine and Corneille (*El Cid*). The great French novelists include Andre Gide, Honore de Balzac (*Cousin Bette*), Stendel (*The Red and the Black*), the father/son duo of Alexandre Dumas (*The Three Musketeers* and *The Man in the Iron Mask*. Victor Hugo is the Charles Dickens of French literature, having penned the masterpieces, *The Hunchback of Notre Dame* and the French national novel, *Les Miserables*. The stream of consciousness of Proust's *Remembrance of Things Past*, and the Absurdist theatre of Samuel Beckett and Eugene Ionesco (*The Rhinoceros*) attest to the groundbreaking genius of the French writers.

Spain

Spain's great writers include Miguel de Cervantes (*Don Quixote*) and Juan Ramon Jimenez. The anonymous national epic, *El Cid*, has been translated into many languages.

Italy

Italy's greatest writers include Virgil, who wrote the great epic, *The Aeneid*; Giovanni Boccaccio (*The Decameron*); and Dante Alighieri (*The Divine Comedy*).

Ancient Greece

Greece will always be foremost in literary assessments due to Homer's epics, *The Iliad* and *The Odyssey*. No one, except Shakespeare, is more often cited. Add to these the works of Plato and Aristotle for philosophy; the dramatists Aeschylus, Euripides, and Sophocles for tragedy, and Aristophanes for comedy. Greece is the cradle not only of democracy, but of literature as well.

Far East

The classical Age of Japanese literary achievement includes the father Kiyotsugu Kanami and the son Motokkiyo Zeami who developed the theatrical experience known as No drama, to its highest aesthetic degree. The son is said to have authored over 200 plays, of which 100 still are extant.

Katai Tayama (*The Quilt*) is touted as the father of the genre known as the Japanese confessional novel. He also wrote in the "ism" of naturalism. His works are definitely not for the squeamish.

The "slice of life" psychological writings of Ryunosuke Akutagawa gained him acclaim in the western world. His short stories, especially "Rashamon" and "In a Grove," are greatly praised for style as well as content.

China, too, has given to the literary world. Li Po, the T'ang dynasty poet from the Chinese Golden Age, revealed his interest in folklore by preserving the folk songs and mythology of China. Po further allows his reader to enter into the Chinese philosophy of Taoism and to know this feeling against expansionism during the T'ang dynastic rule. Back to the T'ang dynasty, which was one of great diversity in the arts, the Chinese version of a short story was created with the help of Jiang Fang. His themes often express love between a man and a woman.

North American Literature

North Americam literature is divided between the United States, Canada, and Mexico. The American writers have been amply discussed in 22.1. Canadian writers of note include feminist Margaret Atwood, (*The Hand Maiden's Tale*); Alice Munro, a remarkable short story writer; and W. P. Kinsella, another short story writer whose two major subjects are North American Indians and baseball. Mexican writers include 1990 Nobel Prize winning poet, Octavio Paz, (The Labyrinth of Solitude) and feminist Rosarian Castillanos (The Nine Guardians).

Africa

African literary greats include South Africans Nadine Gordimer (Nobel Prize for literature) and Peter Abrahams (*Tell Freedom: Memories of Africa*), an autobiography of life in Johannesburg. Chinua Achebe (*Things Fall Apart*) and the poet, Wole Soyinka, hail from Nigeria. Mark Mathabane wrote an autobiography *Kaffir Boy* about growing up in South Africa. Egyptian writer, Naguib Mahfouz, and Doris Lessing from Rhodesia, now Zimbabwe, write about race relations in their respective countries. Because of her radical politics, Lessing was banned from her homeland and The Union of South Africa, as was Alan Paton whose seemingly simple story, *Cry, the Beloved Country*, brought the plight of blacks and the whites' fear of blacks under apartheid to the rest of the world.

Central American/Caribbean Literature

The Caribbean and Central America encompass a vast area and cultures that reflect oppression and colonialism by England, Spain, Portugal, France, and The Netherlands. The Caribbean writers include Samuel Selvon from Trinidad and Armado Valladres of Cuba. Central American authors include dramatist Carlos Solorzano, from Guatemala, whose plays include *Dona Beatriz, The Hapless, The Magician,* and *The Hands of God.*

South American Literature

Chilean Gabriela Mistral was the first Latin American writer to win the Nobel Prize for literature. She is best known for her collections of poetry, *Desolation and Feeling*. Chile was also home to Pablo Neruda, who, in 1971, also won the Nobel Prize for literature for his poetry. His 29 volumes of poetry have been translated into more than 60 languages, attesting to his universal appeal. *Twenty Love Poems* and *Song of Despair* are justly famous. Isabel Allende is carrying on the Chilean literary standards with her acclaimed novel, *House of Spirits*. Argentine Jorge Luis Borges is considered by many literary critics to be the most important writer of his century from South America. His collections of short stories, *Ficciones*, brought him universal recognition. Also from Argentina, Silvina Ocampo, a collaborator with Borges on a collection of poetry, is famed for her poetry and short story collections, which include *The Fury* and *The Days of the Night*.

Noncontinental European Literature

Horacio Quiroga represents Uruguay, and Brazil has Joao Guimaraes Rosa, whose novel, *The Devil to Pay*, is considered first-rank world literature.

Russian Literature

Boris Pasternak won the Nobel Prize (*Dr. Zhivago*). Aleksandr Solzhenitsyn (*The Gulag Archipelago*) is only recently back in Russia after years of expatriation in Vermont. Ilya Varshavsky, who creates fictional societies that are dystopias, or the opposite of utopias, represents the genre of science fiction.

French Literature

French literature is defined by the existentialism of Jean-Paul Sartre (*No Exit, The Flies, Nausea*), Andre Malraux, (*The Fall*), and Albert Camus (*The Stranger, The Plague*), the recipient of the 1957 Nobel Prize for literature. Feminist writings include those of Sidonie-Gabrielle Colette, known for her short stories and novels, as well as Simone de Beauvoir.

Slavic nations

Austrian writer Franz Kafka (*The Metamorphosis, The Trial,* and *The Castle*) is considered by many to be the literary voice of the first-half of the twentieth century. Representing the Czech Republic is the poet Vaclav Havel. Slovakia has dramatist Karel Capek (*R.U.R.*) Romania is represented by Elie Weisel (*Night*), a Nobel Prize winner.

Far East Literature

Asia has many modern writers who are being translated for the western reading public. India's Krishan Chandar has authored more than 300 stories. Rabindranath Tagore won the Nobel Prize for literature in 1913 (*Song Offerings*). Narayan, India's most famous writer (*The Guide*), is highly interested in mythology and legends of India. Santha Rama Rau's work, *Gifts of Passage*, is her true story of life in a British school where she tries to preserve her Indian culture and traditional home.

Revered as Japan's most famous female author, Fumiko Hayashi (*Drifting Clouds*) by the time of her death had written more than 270 literary works.

In 1968 the Nobel Prize for literature was awarded to Yasunari Kawabata (*The Sound of the Mountain, The Snow Country*) considered to be his masterpieces. His Palm-of-the-Hand Stories take the essentials of Haiku poetry and transform them into the short story genre.

Modern feminist and political concerns are written eloquently by Ting Ling, who used the pseudonym Chiang Ping-Chih. Her stories reflect her concerns about social injustice and her commitment to the women's movement.

Skill 20.2 **Analyze in passage context significant themes and genres in American, British, and world literature.**

An archetype is an idealized model of a person, object, or concept from which similar instances are derived, copied, patterned, or emulated. In psychology, an archetype is a model of a person, personality or behavior. Archetypes often appear in literature. William Shakespeare, for example, is known for popularizing many archetypal characters. Although he based many of his characters on existing archetypes from fables and myths, Shakespeare's characters stand out as original by their contrast against a complex, social literary landscape. An image, character, or pattern of circumstances that reoccurs frequently in literature can be considered an archetype.

For example, *Oedipus Rex* has a structure that appears to be repeated in the lives of all men in the sense that all sons are replacements for their fathers. Faulkner, in "Barn Burning" provides an original example that calls forth this archetype.

There are many archetypes, and skillful and creative writers often rely on them to create successful fiction. Some examples of **action archetypes**:

- The search for the killer
- The search for salvation (or the holy grail)
- The search for the hero
- The descent into hell

Some examples of **character archetypes**:
- The double
- The scapegoat
- The prodigal son
- The Madonna and the Magdalene

The family has often been used as a recurring archetypal theme in literature including the Greek play *Oedipus Rex* and other Greek literature such as the *Medea*. Many of Shakespeare's plays also used this archetype: *Hamlet, Romeo and Juliet,* and *King Lear,* for example. Modern writers also use the family archetype, such as *Desire Under the Elms* by Eugene O'Neill and *A Streetcar Named Desire* by Tennessee Williams. Toni Morrison in her popular novel *Beloved* uses the archetype of family by chronicling the difficulties the protagonist Sethe and her family face before the Civil War as well as during the conflict and afterward. The result is a compelling picture of a family's response to the devastation brought on by slavery.

Herman Melville was born in 1819 and grew up in upper-class New York neighborhoods. His mother was a strict Calvinist Presbyterian and had strong views regarding proper behavior. Herman tended to be a rebellious sort, and to some extent his conflicts regarding his mother's viewpoints were never resolved.

When Herman was eleven years old, his father's business failed, and he died shortly afterward. Herman tried working in business for awhile but soon decided he wanted to go to sea.

Working on ships and traveling, he began to write non-fictional pieces about his experiences. In July of 1851, he wrote his most famous work, *Moby Dick*. Before he died, he wrote poems and another well-known novel, *Billy Budd*, which was not published until 1924. Just as he began to write *Moby Dick*, he became friends with Nathaniel Hawthorne, who happened to be his neighbor. Hawthorne's works and friendship became an important influence on his writing.

In *Moby Dick*, the style is indicative of the reportorial writing of the earlier period; however, it is far more than that. It is seen as a great American epic, even though it is not poetry. It was not successful while its author was alive. Its success came much later.

Some Themes:

- Man in conflict with the natural world
- Religion and God's role in the universe
- Good and evil
- Cause and effect
- Duty
- Conscience

Richard Wright was the grandson of slaves and grew up in a time when the lives of African-Americans tended to be very grim. His response to life lived so close to those who had so recently risen from bondage permeates his writing.

His writing went through many changes just as his response to the special reality of life as a black person in a white-dominated world went through many changes. In order to understand his work, the date of the writing—the stage he was undergoing at the time—is very important. He was influenced early by Maxim Gorky, whose own life experience had similarities to Wright's own. Later, he was heavily influenced by Dostoevsky and that writer's themes can be identified in the work from his last period.

Survival for many blacks and black communities required conformity to whatever white people demanded, and Wright rejected that. He felt profoundly alienated and felt that his individuality had been wounded. He became a proletarian revolutionary artist in the earliest years of his career. The American Communist Party nabbed him as their most illustrious recruit to the newly-established literary standards of proletarian realism. He rejected the "conspicuous ornamentation" of institutions imposed by segregation such as the Harlem Renaissance. At the same time, he felt that consciousness must draw its strength from the lore of a great people, his own. He sought, in the early years of the 20th century, to integrate the progressive aspects of the folk culture of the African-Americans into a collective myth that would promote a revolutionary approach to reality.

He left the Communist Party in 1944, largely as a result of his own evolution. *Black Boy*, an autobiographical account of his childhood and young manhood, appeared in 1945. He settled in Paris as a permanent expatriate shortly after its publication. His first stories—*Uncle Tom's Children*—are a re-conception of negro spirituals and black Christianity in which the hero chooses to risk martyrdom in progressively more elevated stages of class consciousness.

Some themes:

- The environment of the South is too small to nourish human beings, especially African-Americans
- Rejection of black militancy
- Violent, battered childhood and victorious adulthood
- Suffocation of instinct and stifling of potential
- Mature reminiscences of a battered childhood
- Black mother's protective nurture and the trauma of an absent or impotent father
- Each is responsible for everyone and everything (later works)

His technique and style are not as important as the impact his ideas and attitudes have had on American life. He set out to portray African-Americans to white readers in such a way that the myth of the uncomplaining, comic, obsequious black man might be replaced.

Willa Cather grew up on the western plains in Nebraska, and much of her best fiction focuses on the pioneering period in that part of the country. She was born in Virginia in 1873 on her family's farm; but in 1884, the family moved to Nebraska where other relatives had settled. Much of the lore that is the basis of her stories came from her visits with immigrant farm women around Red Cloud, where the family eventually made their home.

When she was sixteen, she enrolled at the University of Nebraska in Lincoln where an essay in her English class was favorably accepted and she began to support herself as a journalist. She moved to Pittsburgh and was working as a writer and editor when she decided that she wanted to teach school. Even so, she continued to develop her writing career. On a trip back to Nebraska, she witnessed a wheat harvest, which triggered her motive for writing about the pioneer period of American history.

Some Themes:

- The American Dream
- Prejudice
- Coming of Age
- Nostalgia

Maxine Hong Kingston's parents were Chinese immigrants who lived in Stockton, California. Her fiction is highly autobiographical, and she weaves Chinese myths and fictionalized history with the aim of exploring the conflicts between cultures faced by Chinese-Americans. Her writing exposes the ordeals of the Chinese immigrants who were so exploited by American companies, particularly railroad and agriculture industries. She also explores relationships within the Chinese families, particularly between parents who were born in China and children who were born in America. In a 1980 *New York Times Book Review* interview, she said "What I am doing in this new book [*China Men*] is churning America."

Some Themes:

- Discovery
- The American Dream
- Male/Female Roles
- Metamorphosis
- Enforced Muteness
- Vocal Expression
- Family

Poets:

Walt Whitman's poetry was more often than not inspired by the Civil War. He is America's greatest romantic poet and many of his poems are related to and come directly from the conflict between the northern and southern states. This is not to say that the war was the only influence; he wrote many poems on topics that are not directly related to it. His major work, *Leaves of Grass,* was revised nine times, the last in 1892 shortly before he died. He used sophisticated linguistic devices much ahead of his time. Even though he dealt with a vast, panoramic vision, his style has a personal and immediate effect on the reader.

When he was born in 1819 on Long Island in New York, it was a time of great patriotism for the new nation; however, he experienced the conflict that presented a serious threat to its survival in the war between the states, and it's no wonder that the conflict became the subject matter for most of his creative output. His father was a carpenter and then a farmer. Walt was the second-born of eight, the first son. He had six years of public education before he went to work for Brooklyn lawyers and began to educate himself in the library. He began his writing career with newspaper articles and eventually wrote short stories that were published in newspapers. His unconventional techniques were his own creation and in *Leaves of Grass* he intended to speak for all Americans.

He worked as a volunteer in hospitals to help care for soldiers, and was deeply affected by the horrors of war that he saw first-hand. His poetry was considered to be indecent by some, and he was both praised and vilified during his lifetime. He died in 1892 of tuberculosis.

Some Themes:
- Imagination vs. Scientific Process
- Individualism

Emily Dickinson has been called the "myth of Amherst" because so little is known of her. She was born in 1830, the second child of Edward and Emily Dickinson. Her family was prominent in Massachusetts and played a major role in the founding of Amherst College. Her father's stern, puritanical control of his family played a pivotal role in the poetry that his daughter eventually wrote. Although he was severe and controlling, he saw that his daughters got a good education. Emily attended Amherst Academy and then Mount Holyoke Female Seminary. She obtained a copy of Emerson's poems in 1850 and began to develop her own beliefs regarding religion and the severe God that her father represented.

Only a few of her poems were published during her lifetime, and she was unknown until after her death. After she withdrew from school, she became more and more reclusive and after the death of her father in 1874, she never again left her home. She died of Bright's disease in 1886. Her sister Lavinia found roughly 2,000 poems on small pieces of paper, which were published in several editions. The first full three-volume edition was released in 1955. She has come to be known for her superb use of concrete language and imagery to express and evoke abstract issues. Most people have a favorite Dickinson poem.

Her themes range widely, but following are a few:

- Sanity/insanity
- Doubt
- Death
- Individuality
- Defiance
- Feminism

Gwendolyn Brooks was the first African American to receive a Pulitzer Prize for Poetry with her acute images of African Americans in the cities of America. Born in 1917 to a schoolteacher and a janitor, she grew up in Chicago. She was named poet laureate of Illinois in 1978 and was the first black woman honorary fellow of the Modern Language Association. Her family was close-knit, and she tended to spend her time reading when she was a child. She began writing poems when she was very young. She has also had a successful teaching career at several universities including City University of New York where she was Distinguished Professor. Gwendolyn was writing about the experience of being black long before it became main-stream. She underwent an evolution in subject matter and thinking about being black as a result of the movement of the sixties toward the validity of African Americans. She died of cancer in 2000. She was eighty-three years old.

Themes:

- Poverty and Racism
- Self-respect
- Heritage
- Community
- Family
- Black Unity
- The Basic Humanness in Everyone
- Black Solidarity
- Pride

Leslie Marmon Silko is a Laguna Indian of mixed ancestry that includes Cherokee, German, English, Mexican, and Pueblo. There were several remarkable women in her life, grandmothers and aunts, who taught her the traditions and stories of the Pueblo. At the same time, her father's role in his tribe also made her aware of the abuses her people had experienced at the hands of the government. The major issue was the land that had been stolen from her people. She believed that she could change things by writing about them.

Some themes:

- Evil
- Reciprocity
- Individual/Community
- Native American Traditions
- Native American Religion
- Mixed Breeds
- Scapegoats
- Racism
- Prejudice

Skill 20.3   **Recognize major characteristics and themes of multicultural literature written in the United States.**

American Indian Literature

The foundation of American Indian writing is found in story-telling, oratory, autobiographical and historical accounts of tribal village life, reverence for the environment, and the postulation that the earth with all of its beauty was given in trust, to be cared for and passed on to future generations.

Early American Indian writings

Barland, Hal. *When The Legends Die*

Barrett, S.M. Editor: *Geronimo: His Own Story - Apache*

Eastman, C. & Eastman E. *Wigwam Evenings: Sioux Folktales Retold*

Riggs, L. *Cherokee Night* - drama

Twentieth Century Writers

Deloria, V. *Custer Died for your Sins* (Sioux)

Dorris, M. *The Broken Cord: A Family's on-going struggle with fetal alcohol syndrome* (Modoc)

Hogan, L. *Mean Spirited* (Chickasaw)

Taylor, C.F. *Native American Myths and Legends*

Afro-American Literature

The three phases of Afro-American Literature can be broken down as follows:

- Oppression, slavery, and the re-construction of the post-Civil War/rural South

- Inner city strife/single parenting, drug abuse, lack of educational opportunities and work advancement etc. that was controlled by biased and disinterested factions of society.

- Post-Civil Rights and the emergence of the BLACK movement focusing on biographical and autobiographical Black heroes and their contribution to Black and American culture.

Resources:

1. Pre-Civil War

Bethune, Mary McLoed. *Voice of Black Hope*
Fast, Howard. *Freedom Ride*
Haskins, James. *Black Music in America - A History through its People*
Huggins, Nathan Irving. *Black Odyssey*
Lemann, Nicolas. *The Promised Land*
Stowe, Harriet Beecher. *Uncle Tom's Cabin*
Wheatley, Phyllis. *Memoirs and Poems*

2. Post-Civil War and Reconstruction

Armstrong, William. *Sounder*
Bonham, Frank. *Durango Street*
Childress, Alice. *A Hero Ain't Nothin' But a Sandwich*
Gaines, Ernest. *The Autobiography of Miss Jane Pittman*

3. Post Civil War - Present

Angelou, Maya. *I Know Why the Caged Bird Sings*
Baldwin, James. *Go Tell It on the Mountain*
Haley, Alex. *Roots*
Hansberry, Lorraine. *A Raisin in the Sun*
Lee, Harper. *To Kill a Mockingbird*
Hughes, Langston. *I, Too, Sing America*
Wright, Richard. *White Man Listen!* and *Native Son*

Latino/a Literature

In the field of literature, we have two new expanding areas, Latino/a and feminist writers. These authors write to retain cultural heritage, share their people's struggle for recognition, independence, and survival, and express their hopes for the future.

Latino/Latina Writers
De Cervantes, Lora (Chicana). *Starfish*
Cisneros, Sandra (Hispanic). *Red Sweater* and other short story collections
Marquez, Gabriel Garcia (Colombian). *Hundred Years of Solitude*
Nunoz, A. Lopez (Spanish). *Programas Para Dias Especiales*
Neruda, Pablo (Chile). Nobel Prize Winner- Collections of Poetry
Silko, Leslie Marmon (Mexican). *The Time We Climbed Snake Mountain*
Soto, Gary (Mexican). *The Tales of Sunlight*

Feminist / gender concern literature written by women in the United States

Edith Wharton's *Ethan Frome* is a heartbreaking tale of lack of communication, lack of funds, the unrelenting cold of the Massachusetts winter, and a toboggan ride which gnarls Ethan and Mattie just like the old tree which they smash into. The *Age of Innocence*, in contrast to *Ethan Frome*, is set in the upper echelons of fin-de-siècle New York and explores marriage without stifling social protocols.

Willa Cather's work moves the reader to the prairies of Nebraska and the harsh eking out of existence by the immigrant families who choose to stay there and farm. Her most acclaimed works include *My Antonia* and *Death Comes for the Archbishop*.

Kate Chopin's regionalism and local color takes her readers to the upper-crust Creole society of New Orleans and resort isles off the Louisiana coast. "The Story of an Hour" is lauded as one of the greatest of all short stories. Her feminist liberation novel, *The Awakening*, is still hotly debated.

Eudora Welty's regionalism and dialect shine in her short stories of rural Mississippi, especially in "The Worn Path."

Modern black female writers who explore the world of feminist/gender issues as well as class prohibitions are Alice Walker -- (*The Color Purple*), Zora Neale Hurston (*Their Eyes Were Watching God*), and Toni Morrison (*Beloved*, *Jazz*, and *Song of Solomon*).

Feminists

Alcott, Louisa May. *Little Women*
Friedan, Betty. *The Feminine Mystique: The Second Stage*
Bronte, Charlotte. *Jane Eyre*
Hurston, Zora Neale. *Their Eyes Were Watching God*
Janeway, Elizabeth. *Woman's World, Woman's Place: A Study in Social Mythology*
Chopin, Kate. *The Awakening*
Rich, Adrienne. Arienne Rich's Poetry: *Motherhood As Experience* and *Driving into the Wreck*
Woolf, Virginia. *A Room of One's Own*

DOMAIN V. LANGUAGE AND INTERDISCIPLINARY LANGUAGE ARTS

COMPETENCY 21.0 UNDERSTAND THE HISTORICAL, SOCIAL, CULTURAL, AND TECHNOLOGICAL INFLUENCES SHAPING THE ENGLISH LANGUAGE

Skill 21.1 Analyze the significance of historical events that have influences the development of the English language.

The reign of Elizabeth I ushered in a renaissance that led to the end of the medieval age. It was a very fertile literary period. The exploration of the new world expanded the vision of all levels of the social order from royalty to peasant, and the rejection of Catholicism by many in favor of a Christianity of their own opened up whole new vistas to thought and daily life. The manufacture of cloth had increased, driving many people from the countryside into the cities, and the population of London exploded, creating a metropolitan business center. Printing had been brought to England by William Caxton in the 1470s, and literacy increased from 30% in the 15th century to over 60% by 1530. These seem dramatic changes, and they were, but they were occurring gradually.

The Italian renaissance had a great influence on the renaissance in England, and early in the 16th century most written works were in Latin. It was assumed that a learned person must express his thoughts in that language. However, there began to emerge a determination that vernacular English was valuable in writing, and it began to be defended. Elizabeth's tutor, Roger Ascham, for example, wrote in English.

Luther's thesis in 1517, which brought on the Reformation—an attempt to return to pure Christianity—brought on the breakup of western Christendom and eventually the secularization of society and the establishment of the king or queen as the head of this new/old church. This also brought about a new feeling that being religious was also being patriotic; it promoted nationalism.

The ascension of Elizabeth to the throne also followed a very turbulent period regarding succession, and she ruled for 45 peaceful years, which allowed arts and literature to flourish. Although she, herself, was headstrong and difficult, she happened to have very shrewd political instincts and entrusted power to solid, talented men, most particularly Cecil, her Secretary. and Walsingham, whom she put in charge of foreign policy. She identified with her country as no previous ruler had and that, in itself, brought on a period of intense nationalism. She was a symbol of Englishness. The defeat of the Spanish armada in 1588 was the direct result of the strong support she had from her own nation.

Drama was the principal form of literature in this age. Religious plays had been a part of the life of England for a long time, particularly the courtly life. But in the Elizabethan age, they became more and more secular and were created primarily for courtly entertainment. By the '60s, Latin drama, particularly the tragedies of Seneca and the comedies of Plautus and Terence began to wield an influence in England.

Courtyards of inns became favorite places for the presentation of plays; but in 1576, the Earl of Leicester's Men constructed their own building outside the city and called it The Theatre. Other theatres followed. Each had its own repertory company, and performances were for profit but also for the queen and her court. It is said that Shakespeare wrote *The Merry Wives of Windsor* at the specific command of the queen, who liked Falstaff and wanted to see him in love. It was also for the courtly audience that poetry was introduced into drama.

Shakespeare and Marlowe dominated the '80s and '90s; and at the turn of the century, only a few years before Elizabeth's death, Ben Jonson began writing his series of satirical comedies.

Court favor was notoriously precarious and depended on the whims of the queen and others. Much of the satire of the period reflects the disappointment of writers like Edmund Spenser and John Lyly and the superficiality and treachery of the court atmosphere. "A thousand hopes, but all nothing," wrote Lyly, "a hundred promises, but yet nothing."

Not all literature was dictated by the court. The middle classes were developing and had their own style. Thomas Heywood and Thomas Deloney catered to bourgeois tastes.

The two universities were also sources for the production of literature. The primary aim of the colleges was to develop ministers since there was a shortage brought on by the break with the Catholic Church. However, most university men couldn't make livings as ministers or academics, so they wrote as a way of earning income. Nashe, Marlowe, Robert Greene, and George Peele all reveal in their writings how difficult this path was. Remuneration came mostly from patrons. Greene had sixteen different patrons from seventeen books whereas Shakespeare had a satisfactory relationship with the Earl of Southampton and didn't need to seek other support. Publishers would also sometimes pay for a manuscript, which they would then own. Unfortunately, if the manuscript did not pass muster with all who could condemn it—the court, the religious leaders, prominent citizens—it was the author who was on the hot seat. Very few became as comfortable as Shakespeare did. His success was not only in writing, however, but also from his business acumen.

Writing was seen more as a craft than as an art in this period. There was not great conflict between art and nature, little distinction between literature, sports of the field, or the arts of the kitchen.

Balance and control were important in the England of this day, and this is reflected in the writing, the poetry in particular. The sestina, a form in which the last words of each line in the first stanza are repeated in a different order in each of the following stanzas, became very popular. Verse forms range from the extremely simple four-line ballad stanza through the rather complicated form of the sonnet to the elaborate and beautiful eighteen-line stanza of Spenser's *Epithalamion*. Sonnets were called "quatorzains."

The term "sonnet" was used loosely for any short poem. "Quatorzains" are fourteen-line poems in iambic pentameter with elaborate rhyme schemes. However, Chaucer's seven-line rhyme royal stanza also survived in the 16th century. Shakespeare used it in *The Rape of Lucrece*, for example. An innovation was Spenser's nine-line stanza, called the Spenserian stanza, as used in *The Faerie Queene*.

As to themes, some of the darkness of the previous period can still be seen in some Elizabethan literature, for example, Shakespeare's Richard II (III.ii152-70). At the same time, a spirit of joy, gaiety, innocence, and lightheartedness can be seen in much of the most popular literature, and pastoral themes became popular. The theme of the burning desire for conquest and achievement was also significant in Elizabethan thought.

Some important writers of the Elizabethan age:
Sir Thomas More (1478-1535)
Sir Thomas Wyatt the Elder (1503-1542)
Sir Philip Sidney (1554-1586)
Edmund Spenser (1552-1599)
Sir Walter Raleigh (1552-1618)
John Lyly (1554-1606)
George Peele (1556-1596)
Christopher Marlowe (1564-1593)
William Shakespeare (1564-1616)

The Industrial Revolution in England began with the development of the steam engine. However, the steam engine was only one component of the major technological, socioeconomic, and cultural innovations of the early 19th century that began in Britain and spread throughout the world. An economy based on manual labor was replaced by one dominated by industry and the manufacture of machinery. The textile industries also underwent very rapid growth and change. Canals were being built, roads were improving, and railways were being constructed.

Steam power (fueled primarily by coal) and powered machinery (primarily in the manufacture of textiles) drove the remarkable amplification of production capacity. All-metal machine tools had entered the picture by 1820 making it possible to produce more machines.

The date of the Industrial Revolution varies according to how it is viewed. Some say that it broke out in the 1780s and wasn't fully perceived until the 1830s or 1840s. Others maintain that the beginning was earlier, about 1760 and began to manifest visible changes by 1830. The effects spread through western Europe and North America throughout the 19th century, eventually affecting all major countries of the world. The impact on society has been compared to the period when agriculture began to develop and the nomadic lifestyle was abandoned.

The first Industrial Revolution was followed immediately by the Second Industrial Revolution around 1850 when the progress in technology and world economy gained momentum with the introduction of steam-powered ships and railways and eventually the internal combustion engine and electrical power generation.

In terms of what was going on socially, the most noticeable effect was the development of a middle class of industrialists and businessmen and a decline in the landed class of nobility and gentry. While working people had more opportunities for employment in the new mills and factories, working conditions were often less than desirable. Exploiting children for labor wasn't new—it had always existed—but it was more apparent and perhaps more egregious as the need for cheap labor increased. In England, laws regarding employment of children began to be developed in 1833. Another effect of industrialization was the enormous shift from hand-produced goods to machine-produced ones and the loss of jobs among weavers and others, which resulted in violence against the factories and machinery beginning in about 1811.

Eventually, the British government took measures to protect industry. Another effect was the organization of labor. Because laborers were now working together in factories, mines, and mills, they were better able to organize to gain advantages they felt they deserved. Conditions were bad enough in these workplaces that the energy to bring about change was significant and eventually trade unions emerged. Laborers learned quickly to use the weapon of the strike to get what they wanted. The strikes were often violent and while the managers usually gave in to most of the demands made by strikers, the animosity between management and labor was endemic.

The mass migration of rural families into urban areas also resulted in poor living conditions, long work hours, extensive use of children for labor, and a polluted atmosphere.

Another effect of industrialization of society was the separation of husband and wife. One person stayed at home and looked after the home and family and the other went off to work, a very different configuration from an agriculture-based economy where the entire family was usually involved in making a living. Eventually, gender roles began to be defined by the new configuration of labor in this new world order.

The application of industrial processes to printing brought about a great expansion in newspaper and popular book publishing. This, in turn, was followed by rapid increases in literacy and eventually in demands for mass political participation.

Romanticism, the literary, intellectual, and artistic movement that occurred along with the Industrial Movement was actually a response to the increasing mechanization of society, an artistic hostility to what was taking over the world.

Romanticism stressed the importance of nature in art and language in contrast to the monstrous machines and factories. Blake called them the "dark, satanic mills" in his poem, "And Did Those Feet in Ancient Time."

This movement followed on the heels of the Enlightenment period and was, at least in part, a reaction to the aristocratic and political norms of the previous period. Romanticism is sometimes called the Counter-Enlightenment. It stressed strong emotion, made individual imagination the critical authority, and overturned previous social conventions. Nature was important to the Romanticists and it elevated the achievements of misunderstood heroic individuals and artists who participated in altering society.

Some Romantic Writers:
Johann Wolfgang von Goethe
Walter Scott
Ludwig Tieck
E. T. A. Hoffman
William Wordsworth
Samuel Taylor Coleridge
William Blake
Victor Hugo
Alexander Pushkin
Lord Byron
Washington Irving
James Fenimore Cooper
Henry Wadsworth Longfellow
Edgar Allen Poe
Emily Dickinson
John Keats
Percy Bysshe Shelley

World War I, also known as The First World War, the Great War, and The War to End All Wars raged from July 1914 to the final Armistice on November 11, 1918. It was a world conflict between the Allied Powers led by Great Britain, France, Russia, and the United States (after 1917) and The Central Powers, led by the German Empire, the Austro-Hungarian Empire, and the Ottoman Empire. It brought down four great empires: The Austo-Hungarian, German, Ottoman, and Russian. It reconfigured European and Middle Eastern maps.

More than nine million soldiers died on the various battlefields and nearly that many more in the participating countries' home fronts thanks to food shortages and genocide committed under the cover of various civil wars and internal conflicts. However, more people died of the worldwide influenza outbreak at the end of the war and shortly after than died in the hostilities. The unsanitary conditions engendered by the war, severe overcrowding in barracks, wartime propaganda interfering with public health warnings, and migration of so many soldiers around the world contributed to causing the outbreak to become a pandemic.

The precipitating event of World War I was the June 28, 1914, assassination in Sarajevo of Archduke Franz Ferdinand, heir to the Austrian throne. Gavrilo Princip, a member of a group called Young Bosnia, whose aim included the unification of the South Slavs and independence from Austria, was the assassin. However, the real reasons for the war are still being debated. In the late '20s and early '30s people felt that the war was an accident that precipitated events that simply got out of control. This was used as a major argument for the organization of the League of Nations to prevent such a thing from happening in the future.

At the same time, Germany, France, and Russia were involved in war plans that created an atmosphere where generals and planning staffs were anxious the take the initiatives and make their careers. Once mobilization orders were issued, there was no turning back. Communications problems in 1914 also played a role. Telegraphy and ambassadors were the primary forms of communication, which accounted for disastrous delays from hours to even days.

President Wilson blamed the war on militarism. He felt that aristocrats and military elites had too much control in Germany, Russia, and Austria, and that the war was a consequence of their desire for military power and disdain for democracy. Lenin famously asserted that the worldwide system of imperialism was responsible for the war This argument proved persuasive in the immediate wake of the war and was a precipitating factor in the rise of Marxism and Communism.

A proposal to Mexico to join the war against the Allies was exposed in February, 1917, bringing war closer to America. Further U-boat (German submarines) attacks on American merchant ships led to Wilson's request that Congress declare war on Germany, which it did on April 6, 1917. Following the U.S. declaration of war, countries in the Western Hemisphere, Cuba, Panama, Haiti, Brazil, Guatemala, Nicaragua, Costa Rica, and Honduras declared war on Germany. The Dominican Republic, Peru, Uruguay, and Ecuador contented themselves with the severance of relations. The entry of the United States into the war was the turning point. It's doubtful that the Allies would have won without the infusion of money, supplies, armament, and troops from the Western Hemisphere, primarily from the United States.

The experiences of the war led to a sort of collective national trauma afterwards for all the participating countries. The optimism of the 1900s was entirely gone and those who fought in the war became what is known as "the Lost Generation" because they never fully recovered from their experiences. For the next few years memorials continued to be erected in thousands of European villages and towns.

Certainly a sense of disillusionment and cynicism became pronounced, and nihilism became popular. The world had never before witnessed such devastation, and the depiction in newspapers and on movie screens made the horrors more personal. War has always spawned creative bursts, and this one was no exception.

Poetry, stories, and movies proliferated. In fact, it's still a fertile subject for art of all kinds, particularly literature and movies. In 2006, a young director by the name of Paul Gross created, directed, and starred in *Passchendaele* based on the stories told him by his grandfather, who was haunted all his life by his killing of a young German soldier in this War to End All Wars.

Some literature based on World War I:

"The Soldier," poem by Rupert Brooke
Goodbye to All That, autobiography by Robert Graves
"Anthem for Doomed Youth" and "Strange Meeting," poems by Wilfred Owen, published posthumously by Siegfried Sassoon in 1918
"In Flanders Fields," poem by John McCrae
Three Soldiers, novel by John Dos Passos
Journey's End, play by R. C. Sherriff
All Quiet on the Western Front, novel by Erich Maria Remarque
Death of a Hero, novel by Richard Aldington
A Farewell to Arms, novel by Ernest Hemingway
Memoirs of an Infantry Officer, novel by Siegfried Sassoon
Sergeant York, movie directed by Howard Hawks

The dissolution of the British empire, the most extensive empire in world history and for a time the foremost global power, began in 1867 with its transformation into the modern Commonwealth. Dominion status was granted to the self-governing colonies of Canada in 1867, to Australia in 1902, to New Zealand in 1907, to Newfoundland in 1907, and to the newly-created Union of South Africa in 1910. Leaders of the new states joined with British statesmen in periodic Colonial Conferences, the first of which was held in London in 1887.

The foreign relations of the Dominions were conducted through the Foreign Office of the United Kingdom. Although Canada created a Department of External Affairs in 1909, diplomatic relations with other governments continued to be channeled through the Governors-General, Dominion High Commissioners in London, and British legations abroad. Britain's declaration of war in World War I applied to all of the Dominions, for instance. Even so, the Dominions had substantial freedom in their adoption of foreign policy where this did not explicitly conflict with British interests. The original arrangement of a single imperial military and naval structure became unsustainable as Britain faced new commitments in Europe and the challenge of an emerging German High Seas fleet after 1900, so in 1919 it was decided that the Dominions should have their own navies, reversing a previous agreement that the then Australasian colonies should contribute to the Royal Navy in return for the permanent stationing of a squadron in the region.

The settlement at the end of World War I gave Britain control of Palestine and Iraq after the collapse of the Ottoman Empire in the Middle East.

It also ceded control of the former German colonies of Tanganyika, Southwest Africa (now Namibia), and New Guinea. British zones of occupation in Germany after the war were not considered part of the Empire

Although the Allies won the war and Britain's rule expanded into new areas, the heavy costs of the war made it less and less feasible to maintain the vast empire. Economic losses as well as human losses put increasing pressure on the Empire to give up its far-flung imperial posts in Asia and the African colonies. At the same time, nationalist sentiment was growing in both old and new Imperial territories fueled partly by their troops' contributions to the war and the anger of many non-white ex-servicemen at the racial discrimination they had encountered during their service.

Enthusiasm for the Empire coupled with an increase in nationalism in many of the Dominions came together to create resistance to Britain's intention to take military action against Turkey in 1922.

Full Dominion independence was formalized in the 1926 Balfour Declaration and the 1931 State of Westminster. Each Dominion was henceforth to be equal in status to Britain herself, free of British legislative interference, and autonomous in international relations. The Dominions section created with the Colonial Office in 1907 was upgraded in 1925 to a separate Dominions Office and given its own Secretary of State in 1930.

Canada led the way, becoming the first Dominion to conclude an international treaty entirely independently (1923) and obtaining the appointment (1928) of a British High Commissioner in Ottawa, thereby separating the administrative and diplomatic functions of the Governor-General and ending the latter's anomalous role as the representative of the head of state and of the British Government. Canada's first permanent diplomatic mission to a foreign country opened in Washington, D.C. in 1927. Australia followed in 1940.

Egypt, formally independent by 1922 but bound to Britain by treaty until 1936 and under partial occupation until 1956, similarly severed all constitutional links with Britain. Iraq, which became a British Protectorate in 1922, also gained complete independence in 1932.

In 1948, Ireland became a republic, fully independent from the United Kingdom, and withdrew from the Commonwealth. Ireland's constitution claimed the six counties of Northern Ireland as a part of the Republic of Ireland until 1998. The issue over whether Northern Ireland should remain in the United Kingdom or join the Republic of Ireland has divided Northern Ireland's people and led to a long and bloody conflict known as the Troubles. However, the Good Friday Agreement of 1998 brought about a ceasefire between most of the major organizations on both sides, creating hope for a peaceful resolution.

The rise of anti-colonial nationalist movements in the subject territories and the changing economic situation of the world in the first half of the 20th century challenged an imperial power now increasingly preoccupied with issues nearer home. The Empire's end began with the onset of the Second World War when a deal was reached between the British government and the Indian independence movement whereby India would cooperate and remain loyal during the war but after which they would be granted independence. Following India's lead, nearly all of the other colonies would become independent over the next two decades.

In the Caribbean, Africa, Asia, and the Pacific, post-war decolonization was achieved with almost unseemly haste in the face of increasingly powerful nationalist movements, and Britain rarely fought to retain any territory.

Some Representative Literature:

Heart of Darkness, novel by Joseph Conrad
Passage to India novel by E. M. Forster
"Gunga Din," poem by Rudyard Kipling

History of the English Language

English is an Indo-European language that evolved through several periods. The origin of English dates to the settlement of the British Isles in the fifth and sixth centuries by Germanic tribes called the Angles, Saxons, and Jutes. The original Britons spoke a Celtic tongue while the Angles spoke a Germanic dialect. Modern English derives from the speech of the Anglo-Saxons who imposed not only their language but also their social customs and laws on their new land. From the fifth to the tenth century, Britain's language was the tongue we now refer to as Old English. During the next four centuries, the many French attempts at English conquest introduced many French words to English. However, the grammar and syntax of the language remained Germanic.

Middle English, most evident in the writings of Geoffrey Chaucer, dates loosely from 1066 to 1509. William Caxton brought the printing press to England in 1474 and increased literacy. Old English words required numerous inflections to indicate noun cases and plurals as well as verb conjugations. Middle English continued the use of many inflections and pronunciations that treated these inflections as separately pronounced syllables. English in 1300 would have been written "Olde Anglishe" with the *e*'s at the ends of the words pronounced as our short *a* vowel. Even adjectives had plural inflections: "long dai" became "longe daies" pronounced "long-a day-as." Spelling was phonetic, thus every vowel had multiple pronunciations, a fact that continues to affect the language.

Modern English dates from the introduction of The Great Vowels Shift because it created guidelines for spelling and pronunciation. Before the printing press, books were copied laboriously by hand; the language was subject to the individual interpretation of the scribes. Printers and subsequently lexicographers like Samuel Johnson and America's Noah Webster influenced the guidelines.

As reading matter was mass produced, the reading public was forced to adopt the speech and writing habits developed by those who wrote and printed books.

Despite many students' insistence to the contrary, Shakespeare's writings are in Modern English. It is important to stress to students that language, like customs, morals, and other social factors, is constantly subject to change. Immigration, inventions, and cataclysmic events change language as much as any other facet of life affected by these changes. The domination of one race or nation over others can change a language significantly. Beginning with the colonization of the New World, English and Spanish became dominant languages in the Western hemisphere. American English today is somewhat different in pronunciation and sometimes vocabulary from British English. The British call a truck a "lorry;" baby carriages a "pram," short for "perambulator;" and an elevator a "lift." There are very few syntactical differences, and even the tonal qualities that were once so clearly different are converging.

Though Modern English is less complex than Middle English, having lost many unnecessary inflections, it is still considered difficult to learn because of its many exceptions to the rules. It has, however, become the world's dominant language by reason of the great political, military, and social power of England from the fifteenth to the nineteenth century and of America in the twentieth century.

Modern inventions - the telephone, phonograph, radio, television, and motion pictures - have especially affected English pronunciation. Regional dialects, once a hindrance to clear understanding, have fewer distinct characteristics. The speakers from different parts of the United States of America can be identified by their accents, but more and more as educators and media personalities stress uniform pronunciations and proper grammar, the differences are diminishing.

The English language has a more extensive vocabulary than any other language. Ours is a language of synonyms, words borrowed from other languages, and coined words - many of them introduced by the rapid expansion of technology.

It is important for students to understand that language is in constant flux. Emphasis should be placed on learning and using language for specific purposes and audiences. Negative criticism of a student's errors in word choice or sentence structures will inhibit creativity. Positive criticism that suggests ways to enhance communication skills will encourage exploration.

Perhaps the most basic principle about language in understanding its changes and variations is a simple one: language inevitably changes over time. If a community that speaks a homogeneous language and dialect are for some reason separated with no contact between the two resulting communities, over a few generations, they will be speaking different dialects and eventually will have difficulty understanding each other.

Language changes in all its manifestations: At the phonetic level, the sounds of a language will change as will its orthography.

The vocabulary level will probably manifest the greatest changes. Changes in syntax are slower and less likely to occur. For example, English has changed in response to the influences of many other languages and cultures as well as internal cultural changes such as the development of the railroad and the computer; however, its syntax still relies on word order—it has not shifted to an inflected system even though many of the cultures that have impacted it do, in fact, have an inflected language, such as Spanish.

The most significance influence on a language is the blending of cultures. The Norman Conquest that brought the English speakers in the British Isles under the rule of French speakers impacted the language, but it's significant that English speakers did not adopt the language of the ruling class—they did not become speakers of French. Even so, many vocabulary items entered the language in that period. The Great Vowel Shift that occurred between the 14th and 16th centuries is somewhat of a mystery although it's generally attributed to the migration to Southeast England following the plague of the black death. The Great Vowel Shift largely accounts for the discrepancy between orthography and speech—the difficult spelling system in modern English.

Colonization of other countries has also brought new vocabulary items into the language. Indian English not only has its own easily recognizable attributes as does Australian and North American, those cultural interactions have added to items in the usages of each other and in the language at large. The fact that English is the most widely spoken and understood language all over the world in the 21st century implies that it is constantly being changed by the globalized world.

Other influences, of course, impact language. The introduction of television and its domination by the United States has had great influence on the English that is spoken and understood all over the world. The same is true of the computerizing of the world (Tom Friedman called it "flattening" in his *The World is Flat: A Brief History of the Twenty-first Century*). New terms have been added, old terms have changed meaning ("mouse," for instance), and nouns have been verbalized.

Skill 21.2   Relate English derivatives and borrowings, including slang terms, to their origins in other languages.

Just as countries and families have histories, so do words. Knowing and understanding the origin of a word, where it has been used down through the years, and the history of its meaning as it has changed is an important component of the writing and language teacher's tool kit. Never in the history of the English language or any other language for that matter have the forms and meanings of words changed so rapidly. When America was settled originally, immigration from many countries made it a "melting pot." Immigration accelerated rapidly within the first hundred years, resulting in pockets of language throughout the country. When trains began to make transportation available and affordable, individuals from those various pockets came in contact with each other, shared vocabularies, and attempted to converse.

TEACHER CERTIFICATION STUDY GUIDE

From that time forward, every generation brought the introduction of a technology that made language interchange not only more possible but more important.

Radio began the trend to standardize dialects. A Bostonian might not be understood by a native of Louisiana, who might not be interested in turning the dial to hear the news or a drama or the advertisements of the vendors that had a vested interest in being heard and understood. Soap and soup producers knew a goldmine when they saw it and created a market for radio announcers and actors who spoke without a pronounced dialect. In return, listeners began to hear the English language in a dialect very different from the one they spoke, and as it settled into their thinking processes, it eventually made its way to their tongues, and spoken English began to lose some of its local peculiarities. It has been a slow process, but most Americans can easily understand other Americans, no matter where they come from. They can even converse with a native of Great Britain with little difficulty. The introduction of television carried the evolution further as did the explosion of electronic communicating devices over the past fifty years.

An excellent example of the changes that have occurred in English is a comparison of Shakespeare's original works with modern translations. Without help, twenty-first-century Americans are unable to read the *Folio*. On the other hand, teachers must constantly be mindful of the vocabularies and etymologies of their students, who are on the receiving end of the escalation brought about by technology and increased global influence and contact.

Skill 21.3　Analyze regional and social variations in language in the United States.

Dialect differences are basically in pronunciation. Bostoners say "pahty" for "party" and Southerners blend words like "you all" into "y'all." Besides the dialect differences already mentioned, the biggest geographical factors in American English stem from minor word choice variances. Depending on the region where you live, when you order a carbonated, syrupy beverage most generically called a soft drink, you might ask for a "soda" in the South, or a "pop" in the Midwest. If you order a soda in New York, then you will get a scoop of ice cream in your soft drink, while in other areas you would have to ask for a "float."

COMPETENCY 22.0 UNDERSTAND FUNDAMENTAL CONCEPTS RELATING TO THE STRUCTURE, ACQUISITION, USE, AND ANALYSIS OF LANGUAGE

Skill 22.1 Distinguish structural features of languages.

Sentence completeness

Avoid fragments and run-on sentences. Recognition of sentence elements necessary to make a complete thought, proper use of independent and dependent clauses (see *Use correct coordination and subordination*), and proper punctuation will correct such errors.

Sentence structure

Recognize simple, compound, complex, and compound-complex sentences. Use dependent (subordinate) and independent clauses correctly to create these sentence structures.

Simple   Joyce wrote a letter.
Compound   Joyce wrote a letter, and Dot drew a picture.
Complex   While Joyce wrote a letter, Dot drew a picture.
Compound/Complex When Mother asked the girls to demonstrate their new-found skills, Joyce wrote a letter, and Dot drew a picture.

Note: Do **not** confuse compound sentence elements with compound sentences.

Simple sentence with compound subject
  <u>Joyce</u> and <u>Dot</u> wrote letters.
  The <u>girl</u> in row three and the <u>boy</u> next to her were passing notes across the aisle.

Simple sentence with compound predicate
  Joyce <u>wrote letters</u> and <u>drew pictures</u>.
  The captain of the high school debate team <u>graduated with honors</u> and <u>studied broadcast journalism in college</u>.

Simple sentence with compound object of preposition
  Coleen graded the students' essays for <u>style</u> and <u>mechanical accuracy</u>.

Skill 22.2 Apply principles of language acquisition and use.

Learning approach

Early theories of language development were formulated from learning theory research. The assumption was that language development evolved from learning the rules of language structures and applying them through imitation and reinforcement.

This approach also assumed that language, cognitive, and social developments were independent of each other. Thus, children were expected to learn language from patterning after adults who spoke and wrote Standard English. No allowance was made for communication through child jargon, idiomatic expressions, or grammatical and mechanical errors resulting from too strict adherence to the rules of inflection (*childs* instead of *children*) or conjugation (*runned* instead of *ran*). No association was made between physical and operational development and language mastery.

Linguistic approach

Studies spearheaded by Noam Chomsky in the 1950s formulated the theory that language ability is innate and develops through natural human maturation as environmental stimuli trigger acquisition of syntactical structures appropriate to each exposure level. The assumption of a hierarchy of syntax downplayed the significance of semantics. Because of the complexity of syntax and the relative speed with which children acquire language, linguists attributed language development to biological rather than cognitive or social influences.

Cognitive approach

Researchers in the 1970s proposed that language knowledge derives from both syntactic and semantic structures. Drawing on the studies of Piaget and other cognitive learning theorists (see Skill 4.7), supporters of the cognitive approach maintained that children acquire knowledge of linguistic structures after they have acquired the cognitive structures necessary to process language. For example, joining words for specific meaning necessitates sensory motor intelligence. The child must be able to coordinate movement and recognize objects before she can identify words to name the objects or word groups to describe the actions performed with those objects.

Adolescents must have developed the mental abilities for <u>organizing concepts as well as concrete operations</u>, <u>predicting outcomes</u>, and <u>theorizing</u> before they can assimilate and verbalize complex sentence structures, choose vocabulary for particular nuances of meaning, and examine semantic structures for tone and manipulative effect.

Sociocognitive approach

Other theorists in the 1970s proposed that language development results from sociolinguistic competence. Language, cognitive, and social knowledge are interactive elements of total human development. Emphasis on verbal communication as the medium for language expression resulted in the inclusion of speech activities in most language arts curricula.

Unlike previous approaches, the sociocognitive allowed that determining the appropriateness of language in given situations for specific listeners is as important as understanding semantic and syntactic structures.

By engaging in conversation, children at all stages of development have opportunities to test their language skills, receive feedback, and make modifications. As a social activity, conversation is as structured by social order as grammar is structured by the rules of syntax. Conversation satisfies the learner's need to be heard and understood and to influence others. Thus, his choices of vocabulary, tone, and content are dictated by his ability to assess the language knowledge of his listeners. He is constantly applying his cognitive skills to using language in a social interaction. If the capacity to acquire language is inborn, without an environment in which to practice language, a child would not pass beyond grunts and gestures as did primitive man.

Of course, the varying degrees of environmental stimuli to which children are exposed at all age levels creates a slower or faster development of language. Some children are prepared to articulate concepts and recognize symbolism by the time they enter fifth grade because they have been exposed to challenging reading and conversations with well-spoken adults at home or in their social groups. Others are still trying to master the sight recognition skills and are not yet ready to combine words in complex patterns.

Concerns for the teacher

Because teachers must, by virtue of tradition and the dictates of the curriculum, teach grammar, usage, and writing as well as reading and later literature, the problem becomes when to teach what to whom. The profusion of approaches to teaching grammar alone are mind-boggling. In the universities, we learn about transformational grammar, stratificational grammar, sectoral grammar, etc. But in practice, most teachers, supported by presentations in textbooks and by the methods they learned themselves, keep coming back to the same traditional prescriptive approach - read and imitate - or structural approach - learn the parts of speech, the parts of sentence, punctuation rules, sentence patterns. After enough of the terminology and rules are stored in the brain, then we learn to write and speak. For some educators, the best solution is the worst - don't teach grammar at all.

The same problems occur in teaching usage. How much can we demand students communicate in only Standard English? Different schools of thought suggest that a study of dialect and idiom and recognition of various jargons is a vital part of language development. Social pressures, especially on students in middle and junior high schools, to be accepted within their peer groups and to speak the non-standard language spoken outside the school make adolescents resistant to the corrective, remedial approach. In many communities where the immigrant populations are high, new words are entering English from other languages even as words and expressions that were common when we were children have become rare or obsolete.

Regardless of differences of opinion concerning language development, it is safe to say that a language arts teacher will be most effective using the styles and approaches with which she is most comfortable.

And, if she subscribes to a student-centered approach, she may find that the students have a lot to teach her and each other. Moffett and Wagner in the Fourth Edition of *Student-centered Language Arts K-12* stress the three I's: individualization, interaction, and integration. Essentially, they are supporting the socio-cognitive approach to language development. By providing an opportunity for the student to select his own activities and resources, his instruction is individualized. By centering on and teaching each other, students are interactive. Finally, by allowing students to synthesize a variety of knowledge structures, they integrate them. The teacher's role becomes that of a facilitator.

Benefits of the socio-cognitive approach

This approach has tended to guide the whole language movement, currently in fashion. Most basal readers utilize an integrated, cross-curricular approach to successful grammar, language, and usage. Reinforcement becomes an intradepartmental responsibility. Language incorporates diction and terminology across the curriculum. Standard usage is encouraged and supported by both the core classroom textbooks and current software for technology. Teachers need to acquaint themselves with the computer capabilities in their school district and at their individual school sites. Advances in new technologies require the teacher to familiarize herself with programs that would serve her students' needs. Students respond enthusiastically to technology. Several highly effective programs are available in various formats to assist students with initial instruction or remediation. Grammar texts, such as the Warriner's series, employ various methods to reach individual learning styles. The school library media center should become a focal point for individual exploration.

Second Language Learners

Students who are raised in homes where English is not the first language and/or where standard English is not spoken, may have difficulty with hearing the difference between similar sounding words like "send" and "sent." Any student who is not in an environment where English phonology operates, may have difficulty perceiving and demonstrating the differences between English language phonemes. If students can not hear the difference between words that "sound the same" like "grow" and "glow," they will be confused when these words appear in a print context. This confusion will of course, sadly, impact their comprehension.

Considerations for teaching to English Language Learners include recognition by the teacher that what works for the English language speaking student from an English language speaking family, does not necessarily work in other languages.

Research recommends that ELL students learn to read initially in their first language. It has been found that a priority for ELL should be learning to speak English before being taught to read English. Research supports oral language development, since it lays the foundation for phonological awareness.

COMPETENCY 23.0 UNDERSTAND THE INTERRELATIONSHIP OF LANGUAGE ARTS SKILLS AND THEIR INTEGRATION WITHIN OTHER CONTENT AREAS

Skill 23.1 Recognize the ways in which reading, writing, listening, and speaking interrelate and mutually influence one another.

See Skill 23.2.

Skill 23.2 Analyze methods of integrating language modes to promote learning.

The last twenty years have seen great change in instruction in the English classroom. Gone are the days when literature is taught on Monday, Wednesday is grammar day and Friday you assign writing. Integrating reading, writing, speaking, listening and viewing allow students to make connections between each aspect of language development during each class.

Suggestions for Integrating Language Arts

- Use prereading activities such as discussion, writing, research, and journals. Use writing to tap into prior knowledge before students read; engage students in class discussions about themes, issues, and ideas explored in journals, predicting the outcome and exploring related information.

- Use prewriting activities such as reading model essays, researching, interviewing others, combining sentences and other prewriting activities. Remember that developing language proficiency is a recursive process and involves practice in reading, writing, thinking, speaking, listening and viewing.

- Create writing activities that are relevant to students by having them write and share with real audiences.

- Connect correctness - including developing skills of conventional usage, spelling, grammar, and punctuation - to the revision and editing stage of writing. Review of mechanics and punctuation can be done with mini-lessons that use sentences from student papers, sentence combining strategies, and modeling passages of skilled writers.

- Connect reading, writing, listening, speaking, and viewing by using literature read as a springboard for a variety of activities.

Skill 23.3   Apply techniques and activities for integrating the language arts with other content areas.

Ideas for Interdisciplinary Classroom Activities:

- Have students produce a newspaper that incorporates many different subject areas (sports, weather, crossword puzzles, books reviews, pictures, poetry, advertisements, etc.).
- Connect each student with an "adoptive grandparent" at a nearby nursing home. Have students write their "grandparent" letters and stories, make timelines of their lives, and learn about life during the time period they grew up in.
- Have students create a Powerpoint presentation on a career they are interested in pursuing. Research pros and cons, salary information, skills necessary for the job, etc.
- Using a book the class is reading as a whole, have students pick out any words they are unfamiliar with. Research the origin of those words, their definitions, and then have them write a creative story using each word.

TEACHER CERTIFICATION EXAM

Sample Test

Essay Question

Read the passage below from *The Diary of Anne Frank* (1947); then complete the exercise that follows.

Written on July 15, 1944, three weeks before the Frank family was arrested by the Nazis, Anne's diary entry explains her worldview and future hopes.

"It's difficult in times like these: ideals, dreams and cherished hopes rise within us, only to be crushed by grim reality. It's a wonder I haven't abandoned all my ideals, they seem so absurd and impractical. Yet I cling to them because I still believe, in spite of everything, that people are truly good at heart.

"It's utterly impossible for me to build my life on a foundation of chaos, suffering and death. I see the world being slowly transformed into a wilderness, I hear the approaching thunder that, one day, will destroy us too, I feel the suffering of millions, And yet, when I look up at the sky, I somehow feel that everything will change for the better, that this cruelty too shall end, that peace and tranquility will return once more. In the meantime, I must hold on to my ideals. Perhaps the day will come when I will be able to realize them!"

Using your knowledge of literature, write a response in which you:

- Compare and contrast Anne's ideals with her awareness of the conditions in which she lives; and
- Discuss how the structure of Anne's writing—her sentences and paragraphs—emphasize the above contrast.

Sample Weak Response

   Anne Frank's ideals in this writing make readers clear on the point that she was strongly against Hitler and the Nazis. You can tell that she knows the Nazis are very dangerous and violent people who cause "the suffering of millions." Otherwise, why would she have written this? This fact of Nazis causing the suffering of millions of people, and killing them, is a large contrast to how much she believes "that people are truly good at heart." Anne Frank is right about her ideals. And that is why her whole book is such a large contrast to the conditions in which she lived in WWII, when everything was going wrong in the world. You can also tell from this passage that she is a lot smarter than Hitler was. That is another big contrast in the book.

   Anne's sentences and paragraphs emphasize the above contrast. They are not fiction; they are her own real thoughts, and these thoughts don't cause "a grim reality" of "cruelty" or the "absurd and impractical" things that she talks about as the war's fault. No, Anne's words cause us to see what is true and real in her art and in her heart. She makes us see that love is not the fiction. Hitler and the Nazis are the ones who make the fiction. We can read this in between the lines, which sometimes has to be done.

   Back when Anne Frank wrote her words down on paper, everything was going wrong around her but she knew what to do, and she did it. She wrote a world classic story about her life. This story is a big contrast to what the Germans were doing.

Sample Strong Response

This excerpt from *The Diary of Anne Frank* reveals the inner strength of a young girl who refuses, despite the wartime violence and danger surrounding her, to let her idealism be overcome by hatred and mass killing. This idealism is reflected, in part, by her emphases on universal human hopes such as peace, tranquility, and goodwill. But Anne Frank is no dreamy Pollyanna. Reflecting on her idealism in the context of the war raging around her, she matter-of-factly writes: "my dreams, they seem so absurd and impractical."

This indicates Anne Frank's awareness of not only her own predicament but of human miseries that extend beyond the immediate circumstances of her life. For elsewhere she writes in a similar vein, "In times like these… I see the world being slowly transformed into a wilderness"; despite her own suffering she can "feel the suffering of millions."

And yet Anne Frank believes, "in spite of everything, that people are truly good at heart." This statement epitomizes the stark existential contrast of her worldview with the wartime reality that ultimately claimed her life.

The statement also exemplifies how Anne's literary form—her syntax and diction—mirror thematic content and contrasts. "In spite of everything," she still believes in people. She can "hear the approaching thunder…yet, when I look up at the sky, I somehow feel that everything will change for the better." At numerous points in this diary entry, first-hand knowledge of violent tragedy stands side-by-side with belief in humanity and human progress.

"I must hold on to my ideals," Anne concludes. "Perhaps the day will come when I'll be able to realize them!" In her diary she has done so, and more.

TEACHER CERTIFICATION EXAM

Multiple Choice

Choose the best answer for each of the questions.

1. Which of the following bits of information best describes the structure of English?

   A. Syntax based on word order
   B. Inflected
   C. Romantic
   D. Orthography is phonetic

2. Which of the following sentences contains an error in agreement?

   A. Jennifer is one of the women who writes for the magazine.
   B. Each one of their sons plays a different sport.
   C. This band has performed at the Odeum many times.
   D. The data are available online at the listed website.

3. Which item below is not a research-based strategy that supports reading?

   A. reading more
   B. reading along with a more proficient reader
   C. reading a passage no more than twice
   D. self-monitoring progress

4. Use the table below to answer the question that follows it.

	Math Usage	General Usage
bi (two)	bilinear	bicycle
	bimodal	biplane
	binomial	bifocals
cent (100)	centimeter	century
	centigram	centigrade
	percent	centipede
circum (around)	circumference	circumnavigate
	circumradius	circumstance
	circumcenter	Circumspect

   Which vocabulary strategy does the table above exemplify?

   A. Frayer method
   B. morphemic analysis
   C. semantic mapping
   D. word mapping

5. What type of comprehension do questions beginnings with "who," "what," "where," or "how" assess?

   A. evaluative
   B. inferential
   C. literal
   D. narrative

MIDDLE LEVEL ENGLISH

6. A teacher has taught his students to self-monitor their reading by locating where in the passage they are having difficulty, identifying the specific problem there, and restating the difficult sentence or passage in their own words. These strategies are examples of

   A. graphic and semantic organizers
   B. metacognition
   C. recognizing story structure
   D. summarizing

7. Which of the following is not true about English?
   A. English is the easiest language to learn.
   B. English is the least inflected language.
   C. English has the most extensive vocabulary of any language.
   D. English originated as a Germanic tongue.

8. Regularly requiring students to practice reading short, instructional-level texts at least three times to a peer and to give and receive peer feedback about these readings mainly addresses which reading skill?

   A. Comprehension
   B. fluency
   C. evaluation
   D. word-solving

9. A figure of speech in which someone absent or something inhuman is addressed as though present and able to respond describes

   A. personification.
   B. synechdoche.
   C. metonymy
   D. apostrophe.

10. A conversation between two or more people is called a/an:

    A. parody.
    B. dialogue.
    C. monologue.
    D. analogy.

11. Computer-assisted instruction (CAI) accommodates all of the following factors in reading instruction *except for*

    A. free-form responses to comprehension questions
    B. increased motivation
    C. the addition of speech with computer-presented text
    D. the use of computers for word processing, and the integration of writing instruction with reading

12. This statement, "I'll die if I don't pass this course," exemplifies a/an:

    A. barbarism.
    B. oxymoron.
    C. hyperbole.
    D. antithesis.

13. The substitution of "went to his rest" for "died" exemplifies a/an

    A. bowdlerism.
    B. jargon.
    C. euphemism.
    D. malapropism.

14. The appearance of a Yankee from Connecticut in the Court of King Arthur is an example of a/an

    A. rhetoric.
    B. parody.
    C. paradox.
    D. anachronism.

15. To explain or to inform belongs in the category of

    A. exposition.
    B. narration.
    C. persuasion.
    D. description.

16. Which of the four underlined sections of the following sentence contains an error that a word processing spellchecker probably wouldn't catch?

    He tuc the hors by the rains and pulled it back to the stabel.

    A. tuc
    B. hors
    C. rains
    D. stabel

17. For students with poor vocabularies, the teacher should recommend first that

    A. they enroll in a Latin class.
    B. they read newspapers, magazines and books on a regular basis.
    C. they write the words repetitively after looking them up in the dictionary.
    D. they use a thesaurus to locate and incorporate the synonyms found there into their vocabularies.

18. *Diction* is best defined as

    A. The specific word choices an author makes in order to create a particular mood or feeling in the reader.
    B. Writing that explains something thoroughly.
    C. The background, or exposition, for a short story or drama.
    D. Word choices that help teach a truth or moral.

19. Before reading a passage, a teacher gives her students an anticipation guide with a list of statements related to the topic they are about to cover in the reading material. She asks the students to indicate their agreement or disagreement with each statement on the guide. This activity is intended to

   A. elicit students' prior knowledge of the topic and set a purpose for reading
   B. help students to identify the main ideas and supporting details in the text
   C. help students to synthesize information from the text
   D. help students to visualize the concepts and terms in the text

20. Varying the complexity of a graphic organizer exemplifies differentiating which aspect of a lesson?

   A. its content/topic
   B. its environment
   C. its process
   D. its product

21. All of the following techniques are used to observe student progress (conduct ongoing informal assessment) except for

   A. analyzing the student work product at key stages
   B. collecting data from assessment tests
   C. posing strategic questions
   D. observing students as they work

22. A paper explaining the relationship between food and weight gain contains the signal words "because," "consequently," "this is how," and "due to." These words suggest that the paper has which text structure?

   A. cause and effect structure
   B. compare and contrast structure
   C. descriptive structure
   D. sequential structure

23. A paper written in first person and having characters, a setting, a plot, some dialogue, and events sequenced chronologically with some flashbacks exemplifies which genre?

   A. exposition
   B. narration
   C. persuasion
   D. speculation

24. Which group of words is not a sentence?

   A. In keeping with the graduation tradition, the students, in spite of the rain, standing in the cafeteria tossing their mortarboards.
   B. Rosa Parks, who refused to give up her seat on the bus, will be forever remembered for her courage.
   C. Taking advantage of the goalie's being out of the net, we scored our last and winning goal.
   D. When it began to rain, we gathered our possessions and ran for the pavilion.

25. "Clean as a whistle" and "easy as falling off a log" exemplify

   A. semantics.
   B. parody.
   C. irony.
   D. clichés.

26. If a student uses slang and expletives, what is the best course of action to take in order to Improve the student's formal Communication skills?

   A. ask the student to rephrase their writing; that is, translate it into language appropriate for the school principal to read.
   B. refuse to read the student's papers until he conforms to a more literate style.
   C. ask the student to read his work aloud to the class for peer evaluation.
   D. rewrite the flagrant passages to show the student the right form of expression.

27. Which of the following is not a theme of Native American writing?

   A. Emphasis on the hardiness of the human body and soul
   B. The strength of multi-cultural assimilation
   C. Indignation about the genocide of native peoples
   D. Remorse for the loss of the Indian way of life

28. Oral debate is most closely associated with which form of discourse?

   A. Description
   B. Exposition
   C. Narration
   D. Persuasion

29. Read the following passage:

"It would have been hard to find a passer-by more wretched in appearance. He was a man of middle height, stout and hardy, in the strength of maturity; he might have been forty-six or seven. A slouched leather cap hid half his face, bronzed by the sun and wind, and dripping with sweat."

What is its main form of discourse?

A. Description
B. Narration
C. Exposition
D. Persuasion

30. The arrangement and relationship of words in sentences or sentence structures best describes

A. style.
B. discourse.
C. thesis.
D. syntax.

31. Identify the sentence that has an error in parallel structure.

A. In order to help your favorite cause, you should contribute time or money, raise awareness, and write congressmen.
B. Many people envision scientists working alone in a laboratory and discovering scientific breakthroughs.
C. Some students prefer watching videos to textbooks because they are used to visual presentation.
D. Tom Hanks, who has won two Academy Awards, is celebrated as an actor, director, and producer.

32. Consider the following sentence:

Mr. Brown is a school volunteer with a reputation and twenty years service.

Which phrase below best represents the logical intent of the underlined phrase above (Choice E is identical to the underlined phrase).

A. with a reputation for twenty years' service
B. with a reputation for twenty year's service
C. who has served twenty years
D. with a service reputation of twenty years

33. Consider the following sentence:

    *Joe **didn't hardly know his cousin Fred**, who'd had a rhinoplasty.*

    Which word group below best conveys the intended meaning of the underlined section above.

    A. hardly did know his cousin Fred
    B. didn't know his cousin Fred hardly
    C. hardly knew his cousin Fred
    D. didn't know his cousin Fred

34. The literary device of personification is used in which example below?

    A. "Beg me no beggary by soul or parents, whining dog!"
    B. "Happiness sped through the halls cajoling as it went."
    C. "O wind thy horn, thou proud fellow."
    D. "And that one talent which is death to hide."

35. Among junior-high school students of low-to-average readability levels which work would most likely stir reading interest?

    A. *Elmer Gantry*, Sinclair Lewis
    B. *Smiley's People*, John LeCarre
    C. *The Outsiders*, S. E. Hinton
    D. *And Then There Were None*, Agatha Christie

36. Consider the following poem:

    My name is John Welington Wells,
    I'm a dealer in magic and spells,
    In blessings and curses,
    And ever-fill'd purses,
    In prophecies, witches, and knells.

    A. sonnet
    B. haiku
    C. limerick
    D. cinquain

37. Which of the following terms does *not* denote a figure of speech (figurative language)?

    A. Simile
    B. Euphemism
    C. Onomatopoeia
    D. Allusion

38. The first African American to receive the Pulitzer Prize for Poetry was

    A. Gwendolyn Brooks
    B. Harriet E. Wilson
    C. Richard Wright
    D. James Edwin Campbell

39. The principal writer of *The Declaration of Independence* was

    A. Patrick Henry
    B. Thomas Jefferson
    C. Ben Franklin
    D. George Washington

40. Pearl appears as an important character in

    A. *The Scarlet Letter*
    B. *Moby Dick*
    C. *The House of the Seven Gables*
    D. "The Cask of Amontillado"

41. The Old English period refers to

    A. The Fourth Century
    B. The Third through the Eighth Century
    C. The Fifth through the Tenth Century
    D. The Fifth through the Eighth Century

42. What factor below introduced Modern English?

    A. The Great Vowel Shift
    B. The printing press
    C. The invasion of the Normans
    D. Phonetic spelling

43. Students are fluent readers if they

    A. read texts with expression or prosody.
    B. read word-to-word and haltingly.
    C. must intentionally decode a majority of the words.
    D. write disorganized sentences

44. Reading assessment should take place

    A. At the end of the semester.
    B. At the end of a unit.
    C. Constantly.
    D. All of the above.

45. Effective assessment requires that

    A. Students not be involved in the assessment process.
    B. Testing activities are kept separate from the teaching activities.
    C. It assess what classroom instruction has prepared the student to read.
    D. Tests, in order to be reliable, should never use materials previously studied in the classroom

46. Effective assessment means that

    A. It ignores age and cultural considerations
    B. Students' weaknesses are emphasized.
    C. Only reading skills count.
    D. It is integrated with instruction and is not intrusive.

47. Which of the following approaches is *not* useful in assessing slower or immature readers?

    A. Repeated readings.
    B. Echo reading.
    C. Wide reading.
    D. Reading content that is more difficult than their skill levels in order to "stretch" their abilities.

48. All of the following concerns would require a teacher to refer them to another resource *except for*

    A. Auditory trauma.
    B. Ear infection.
    C. Vision problems.
    D. Underdeveloped vocabulary.

49. Middle-School students bring little, if any, initial experience in

    A. Phonics.
    B. Phonemics.
    C. Textbook reading assignments.
    D. Stories read by the teacher.

50. To enhance reading comprehension, experts recommend all of these techniques *except for*

    A. Read material through only once, but read slowly and carefully.
    B. Read material through more than once according to a plan.
    C. Create a map for the next reading.
    D. Highlight or take notes during reading.

51. In the hierarchy of needs for adolescents who are becoming more team-oriented in their approach to learning, which need do they exhibit most?

    A. Need for competence
    B. Need for love/acceptance
    C. Need to know
    D. Need to belong

52. What is the best course of action when a child refuses to complete an assignment on the grounds that it is morally objectionable?

   A. Speak with the parents and explain the necessity of studying this work.
   B. Encourage the child to sample some of the text before making a judgment.
   C. Place the child in another teacher's class where students are studying an acceptable work.
   D. Provide the student with alternative material that serves the same curricular purpose.

53. Which of the following responses to literature typically give middle school students the most problems?

   A. Interpretive
   B. Evaluative
   C. Critical
   D. Emotional

54. Overcrowded classes prevent the individual attention needed to facilitate language development. This drawback can be best overcome by

   A. Dividing the class into independent study groups.
   B. Assigning more study time at home.
   C. Using more drill practice in class.
   D. Team teaching.

55. The most significant drawback to applying learning theory research to classroom practice is that

   A. today's students do not acquire reading skills with the same alacrity as when greater emphasis was placed on reading classical literature.
   B. development rates are complicated by geographical and cultural differences that are difficult to overcome.
   C. homogeneous grouping has contributed to faster development of some age groups.
   D. social and environmental conditions have contributed to an escalated maturity level than research done twenty or more years ago would seem to indicate.

56. Modeling is a practice that requires students to

   A. create a style unique to their own language capabilities.
   B. emulate the writing of professionals.
   C. paraphrase passages from good literature.
   D. peer evaluate the writings of other students.

57. **Reading a piece of student writing to assess the overall impression of the product is**

    A. holistic evaluation.
    B. portfolio assessment.
    C. analytical evaluation.
    D. using a performance system.

58. **A formative evaluation of student writing**

    A. requires a thorough marking of mechanical errors with a pencil or pen.
    B. makes comments on the appropriateness of the student's interpretation of the prompt and the degree to which the objective was met.
    C. requires the student to hand in all the materials produced during the process of writing.
    D. involves several careful readings of the text for content, mechanics, spelling, and usage.

50. **Writing ideas quickly without interruption of the flow of thoughts or attention to conventions is called**

    A. brainstorming.
    B. mapping.
    C. listing.
    D. Free writing.

60. **The students in Mrs. Cline's seventh grade language arts class were invited to attend a performance of *Romeo and Juliet* presented by the drama class at the high school. To best prepare, they should**

    A. read the play as a homework exercise.
    B. read a synopsis of the plot and a biographical sketch of the author.
    C. examine a few main selections from the play to become familiar with the language and style of the author.
    D. read a condensed version of the story and practice attentive listening skills.

61. **Which of the following sentences is unambiguously properly punctuated?**

    A. The more you eat; the more you want.
    B. The authors—John Steinbeck, Ernest Hemingway, and William Faulkner—are staples of modern writing in American literature textbooks.
    C. Handling a wild horse, takes a great deal of skill and patience.
    D. The man, who replaced our teacher, is a comedian.

62. In a timed essay test of an hour's duration, how much time should be devoted to prewriting.

    A. five
    B. ten
    C. fifteen
    D. twenty

63. A student informative composition should consist of a minimum of how many paragraphs?

    A. three
    B. four
    C. five
    D. six

64. In 'inverted triangle' introductory paragraphs, the thesis sentence occurs

    A. at the beginning of the paragraph.
    B. in the middle of the paragraph.
    C. at the end of the paragraph.
    D. in the second paragraph.

65. A punctuation mark indicating omission, interrupted thought, or an incomplete statement is a/an
    A. ellipsis.
    B. anachronism.
    C. colloquy.
    D. idiom

66. Which of the following would be the most significant factor in teaching Homer's *Iliad* and *Odyssey* to any particular group of students?

    A. Identifying a translation on the appropriate reading level
    B. Determining the students' interest level
    C. Selecting an appropriate evaluative technique
    D. Determining the scope and delivery methods of background study

67. Which of the following contains an error in possessive punctuation?

    A. Doris's shawl
    B. mother's-in-law frown
    C. children's lunches
    D. ambassador's briefcase

68. Which aspect of language is innate?

    A. Biological capability to articulate sounds understood by other humans
    B. Cognitive ability to create syntactical structures
    C. Capacity for using semantics to convey meaning in a social environment
    D. Ability to vary inflections and accents

69. Written on the sixth grade reading level, most of S. E. Hinton's novels (for instance, *The Outsiders*) have the greatest reader appeal with

    A. sixth graders.
    B. ninth graders.
    C. twelfth graders.
    D. adults.

70. After watching a movie of a train derailment, a child exclaims, "Wow, look how many cars fell off the tracks. There's junk everywhere. The engineer must have really been asleep." Using the facts that the child is impressed by the wreckage and assigns blame to the engineer, a follower of Piaget's theories would estimate the child to be about

    A. ten years old.
    B. twelve years old.
    C. fourteen years old.
    D. sixteen years old.

71. Which of the following should not be included in the opening paragraph of an informative essay?

    A. Thesis sentence
    B. Details and examples supporting the main idea
    C. broad general introduction to the topic
    D. A style and tone that grabs the reader's attention

72. Children's literature became established in the

    A. seventeenth century
    B. eighteenth century
    C. nineteenth century
    D. twentieth century

73. Which of the following is the least effective procedure for promoting consciousness of audience?

    A. Pairing students during the writing process
    B. Reading all rough drafts before the students write the final copies
    C. Having students compose stories or articles for publication in school literary magazines or newspapers
    D. Writing letters to friends or relatives

74. Which of the following is not a technique of prewriting?

    A. Clustering
    B. Listing
    C. Brainstorming
    D. Proofreading

TEACHER CERTIFICATION EXAM

Answer Key

1. A
2. A
3. C
4. B
5. C
6. C
7. A
8. B
9. D
10. B
11. A
12. C
13. C
14. D
15. A
16. C
17. B
18. A
19. A
20. C
21. B
22. A
23. B
24. A
25. D
26. A
27. B
28. D
29. A
30. D
31. C
32. D
33. C
34. B
35. C
36. C
37. D

38. A
39. B
40. A
41. C
42. A
43. A
44. D
45. C
46. D
47. D
48. D
49. C
50. A
51. B
52. D
53. B
54. A
55. D
56. B
57. A
58. B
59. D
60. D
61. B
62. B
63. C
64. C
65. A
66. A
67. B
68. A
69. B
70. A
71. B
72. A
73. B
74. D

TEACHER CERTIFICATION EXAM

Answers with Rationales

1. **Which of the following bits of information best describes the structure of English?**

    A. Syntax based on word order.
    B. Inflected.
    C. Romantic.
    D. Orthography is phonetic.

The correct answer is A. The syntax of English, reflective of its Germanic origins, relies on word order rather than inflection. Because of this and the many influences of other languages (particularly with regard to vocabulary), the orthography is not phonetic, which complicates the teaching of standardized spelling.

2. **Which of the following sentences contains an error in agreement?**

    A. Jennifer is one of the women who writes for the magazine.
    B. Each one of their sons plays a different sport.
    C. This band has performed at the Odeum many times.
    D. The data are available online at the listed website.

The correct answer is A. "Women" is the plural antecedent of the relative pronoun "who," which is functioning as the subject in its clause; so "who" is plural and requires the 3rd person plural form for the verb: "write."

3. **Which item below is not a research-based strategy that supports reading?**

    A. reading more
    B. reading along with a more proficient reader
    C. reading a passage no more than twice
    D. self-monitoring progress

The correct answer is C. Actually, research shows that reading a passage several times improves fluency, and, depending on the complexity of the material, improves comprehension, too. The more complex the material, the more comprehension value in repeated readings.

MIDDLE LEVEL ENGLISH

TEACHER CERTIFICATION EXAM

4. Use the table below to answer the question that follows it.

	Math Usage	General Usage
bi (two)	bilinear	bicycle
	bimodal	biplane
	binomial	bifocals
cent (100)	centimeter	century
	centigram	centigrade
	percent	centipede
circum (around)	circumference	circumnavigate
	circumradius	circumstance
	circumcenter	Circumspect

Which vocabulary strategy does the table above exemplify?

A. Frayer method
B. morphemic analysis
C. semantic mapping
D. word mapping

The answer is B. Morphemes are the smallest units of language that have an associated meaning. The purpose of morphemic analysis is to apply morphemic awareness to the task of learning new words. The Frayer method involves having students use their own words to define new words and to link those definitions to personal experiences. Semantic mapping incorporates graphical clues to concepts and is a subset of graphic organizers. Word mapping is another subset of graphic organizers and consists of displaying such information as the various forms a word may take as it transforms through the parts of speech.

5. **What type of comprehension do questions beginnings with "who," "what," "where," or "how" assess?**

A. evaluative
B. inferential
C. literal
D. narrative

The correct answer is C. Literal questions ask for facts from the reading. The student can put his finger right on the answer and prove that he is correct. These questions are sometimes referred to as "right there" questions. Evaluative questions require a judgement of some sort. Inferential questions ask students to make an educated guess. Narrative questions involve aspects of a story beyond literal considerations.

TEACHER CERTIFICATION EXAM

6. **A teacher has taught his students to self-monitor their reading by locating where in the passage they are having difficulty, by identifying the specific problem there, and by restating the difficult sentence or passage in their own words. These strategies are examples of**

    A. graphic and semantic organizers
    B. metacognition
    C. recognizing story structure
    D. summarizing

The correct answer is C. Good readers use metacognitive strategies (various ways of thinking about thinking) to improve their reading. Before reading, they clarify their purpose for reading and preview the text. During reading, they monitor their understanding, adjusting their reading speed to fit the difficulty of the text and fixing any comprehension problems they have. After reading, they check their understanding of what they read.

7. **Which of the following is not true about English?**

    A. English is the easiest language to learn.
    B. English is the least inflected language.
    C. English has the most extensive vocabulary of any language.
    D. English originated as a Germanic tongue.

The answer is A. English has its own inherent quirks which make it difficult to learn, plus it has incorporated words, ands even structures, from many disparate language groups in its lexicon and syntax. Languages with lexicons limited to words governed by a consistent set of relatively simple rules exist, so English is certainly not the easiest language to learn.

8. **Regularly requiring students to practice reading short, instructional-level texts at least three times to a peer and to give and receive peer feedback about these readings mainly addresses which reading skill?**

    A. Comprehension
    B. fluency
    C. evaluation
    D. word-solving

The correct answer is B. Fluency is the ability to read text quickly with accuracy, phrasing, and expression. Fluency develops over time and requires substantial reading practice. This activity provides just this sort of practice. The peer feedback portion does address comprehension, evaluation, and some word-solving; but the main thrust is on fluency development.

MIDDLE LEVEL ENGLISH

TEACHER CERTIFICATION EXAM

9. A figure of speech in which someone absent or something inhuman is addressed as though present and able to respond describes

    A. personification.
    B. synechdoche.
    C. metonymy
    D. apostrophe.

The answer is D. An apostrophe differs from a personification in the important respect that a "someone" cannot be "personified," plus personifications come in far more varieties than are suggested by the definition in question. A synechdoche is a figure of speech which represents some whole or group by one of its or their parts or members. Metonymy is the substitution of a word for a related word.

10. A conversation between two or more people is called a/an

    A. parody.
    B. dialogue.
    C. monologue.
    D. analogy.

The answer is B. Dialogues are the conversations virtually indispensable to dramatic work, and they often appear in narrative and poetry, as well. A parody is a work that adopts the subject and structure of another work in order to ridicule it. A monologue is a work or part of a work written in the first person. An analogy illustrates an idea by means of a more familiar one that is similar or parallel to it.

11. Computer-assisted instruction (CAI) accommodates all of the following factors in reading instruction _except for_

    A. free-form responses to comprehension questions
    B. increased motivation
    C. the addition of speech with computer-presented text
    D. the use of computers for word processing, and the integration of writing instruction with reading

The correct answer is A. CAI does not accommodate free-form responses to comprehension questions, and relies heavily on drill-and-practice and multiple-choice formats. This is a limitation of CAI.

12. This statement, "I'll die if I don't pass this course," exemplifies a/an

    A. barbarism.
    B. oxymoron.
    C. hyperbole.
    D. antithesis.

The answer is C. A hyperbole is an exaggeration for the sake of emphasis. It is a figure of speech not meant to be taken literally. A barbarism is the use of incorrect or unacceptable language. An oxymoron is a term comprised of opposite or incongruous elements, such as peace fighter.

13. The substitution of "went to his rest" for "died" exemplifies a/an

    A. bowdlerism.
    B. jargon.
    C. euphemism.
    D. malapropism.

The answer is C. A euphemism alludes to a distasteful topic in a pleasant manner in order to obscure or soften the disturbing impact of the original. A bowdlerism is a prudish version of something. Jargon is language specific to some occupation or activity. A Malapropism is the improper use of a word that sounds like the word that would fit the context. The result is most often ludicrous.

14. The appearance of a Yankee from Connecticut in the Court of King Arthur is an example of a/an

    A. rhetoric.
    B. parody.
    C. paradox.
    D. anachronism.

The answer is D. Anachronism is the placing of characters, persons, events or things into time frames incongruent with their actual dates. Parody is poking fun at something. Paradox is a seeming contradiction. Anachronism is something out of time frame.

TEACHER CERTIFICATION EXAM

15. To explain or to inform belongs in the category of

    A. exposition.
    B. narration.
    C. persuasion.
    D. description.

The answer is A. Exposition sets forth a systematic explanation of any subject and informs the audience about various topics. It can also introduce the characters of a story and their situations as the story begins. Narration tells a story. Persuasion seeks to influence an audience so that they will adopt some new point of view or take some action. Description provides sensory details and addresses spatial relationships of objects.

16. Which of the four underlined sections of the following sentence contains an error that a word processing spellchecker probably wouldn't catch?

    He tuc the hors by the rains and pulled it back to the stabel.

    A. tuc
    B. hors
    C. rains
    D. stabel

The correct answer is C. Spellcheckers only catch errors in conventional modern English spelling. They cannot catch errors involving incorrect homophone usage. "Rains" is the only one of the four words to conform to conventional English spelling, but it clearly is not the word called for by the context.

17. For students with poor vocabularies, the teacher should recommend first that

    A. they enroll in a Latin class.
    B. they read newspapers, magazines and books on a regular basis.
    C. they write the words repetitively after looking them up in the dictionary.
    D. they use a thesaurus to locate and incorporate the synonyms found there into their vocabularies.

The answer is B. Regularly reading a wide variety of materials for pleasure and information is the best way to develop a stronger vocabulary. The other suggestions have limited application and do not serve to reinforce an enthusiasm for reading.

MIDDLE LEVEL ENGLISH

TEACHER CERTIFICATION EXAM

18. *Diction* is best defined as

   A. The specific word choices an author makes in order to create a particular mood or feeling in the reader.
   B. Writing that explains something thoroughly.
   C. The background, or exposition, for a short story or drama.
   D. Word choices that help teach a truth or moral.

The answer is A. Diction refers to an author's choice of words, expressions and style to convey his/her meaning. The other choices are only marginally related to this meaning, so the choice is a clear one.

19. **Before reading a passage, a teacher gives her students an anticipation guide with a list of statements related to the topic they are about to cover in the reading material. She asks the students to indicate their agreement or disagreement with each statement on the guide. This activity is intended to**

   A. elicit students' prior knowledge of the topic and set a purpose for reading
   B. help students to identify the main ideas and supporting details in the text
   C. help students to synthesize information from the text
   D. help students to visualize the concepts and terms in the text

The correct answer is A. Establishing a purpose for reading, the foundation for a reading unit or activity, is intimately connected to activating the students' prior knowledge in strategic ways. When the reason for reading is developed in the context of the students' experiences, they are far better prepared to succeed because they can make connections from a base they thoroughly understand. This influences motivation, and with proper motivation, students are more enthused and put forward more effort to understand the text. The other choices are only indirectly supported by this activity and are more specific in focus.

TEACHER CERTIFICATION EXAM

20. Varying the complexity of a graphic organizer exemplifies differentiating which aspect of a lesson?

    A. its content/topic
    B. its environment
    C. its process
    D. its product

The correct answer is C. Differentiating the process means offering a variety of learning activities or strategies to students as they manipulate the ideas embedded within the lesson concept. For example, students may use graphic organizers, maps, diagrams, or charts to display their comprehension of concepts covered. Varying the complexity of a graphic organizer can very effectively accommodate differing levels of cognitive processing so that students of differing ability are appropriately engaged. Lesson topic and content remain the same, the lesson is still taking place in the same environment, and, in most lessons, the graphic organizer is not the product of the lesson.

21. All of the following techniques are used to conduct ongoing informal assessment of student progress except for

    A. analyzing the student work product at key stages
    B. collecting data from assessment tests
    C. posing strategic questions
    D. observing students as they work

The answer is B. The key here hinges on the adjective, "informal." Assessment tests employ standardized materials and formats to monitor student progress and to report it in statistical terms. The other choices are relatively informal, teacher-specific techniques addressing more current-lesson-specific products and dynamics.

22. **A paper explaining the relationship between food and weight gain contains the signal words "because," "consequently," "this is how," and "due to." These words suggest that the paper has which text structure?**

    A. cause and effect structure
    B. compare and contrast structure
    C. descriptive structure
    D. sequential structure

The answer is A. These signal words connect events in a causal chain, creating an explanation of some process or event. Compare and contrast structure presents similarities and differences. Descriptive structure presents a sensory impression of something or someone. Sequential structure references what comes first, next, last, and so on.

23. **A paper written in first person and having characters, a setting, a plot, some dialogue, and events sequenced chronologically with some flashbacks exemplifies which genre?**

    A. exposition
    B. narration
    C. persuasion
    D. speculation

The correct answer is B. Narrative writing tells a story, and all the listed elements pertain to stories. Expository writing explains or informs. Persuasive writing states an opinion and attempts to persuade an audience to accept the opinion or to take some specified action. Speculative writing explores possible developments from given circumstances.

24. **Which group of words is not a sentence?**

    A. In keeping with the graduation tradition, the students, in spite of the rain, standing in the cafeteria tossing their mortarboards.
    B. Rosa Parks, who refused to give up her seat on the bus, will be forever remembered for her courage.
    C. Taking advantage of the goalie's being out of the net, we scored our last and winning goal.
    D. When it began to rain, we gathered our possessions and ran for the pavilion.

The correct answer is A. This is a sentence fragment because sentences require a subject and a verb and there is no verb. Changing "the students, in spite of the rain, standing" to "the students, in spite of the rain, were standing" corrects the problem.

25. "Clean as a whistle" and "easy as falling off a log" exemplify

    A. semantics.
    B. parody.
    C. irony.
    D. clichés.

The answer is D. A cliché is a phrase or expression that has become dull due to overuse. Semantics is a field of language study. Parody is poking fun at something. Irony is using language to create an unexpected or opposite meaning of the literal words being used.

26. If a student uses slang and expletives, what is the best course of action to take in order to improve the student's formal communication skills?

    A. ask the student to rephrase their writing; that is, translate it into language appropriate for the school principal to read.
    B. refuse to read the student's papers until he conforms to a more literate style.
    C. ask the student to read his work aloud to the class for peer evaluation.
    D. rewrite the flagrant passages to show the student the right form of expression.

The answer is A. Asking the student to write to the principal, a respected authority figure, will alert the student to the need to use formal language. Simply refusing to read the paper is not only negative, it also sets up a power struggle. Asking the student to read slang and expletives aloud to the class for peer evaluation is to risk unproductive classroom chaos and to support the class clowns. Rewriting the flagrant passages for the student to model formal expression does not immerse the student in the writing process.

TEACHER CERTIFICATION EXAM

27. Which of the following is not a theme of Native American writing?

- A. Emphasis on the hardiness of the human body and soul
- B. The strength of multi-cultural assimilation
- C. Indignation about the genocide of native peoples
- D. Remorse for the loss of the Indian way of life

The answer is B. Originating in a vast body of oral traditions from as early as before the fifteenth century, Native American literature themes include "nature as sacred," "the interconnectedness of life," "the hardiness of body and soul," "indignation about the destruction of the Native American way of life," and "the genocide of many tribes by the encroaching settlements of European Americans." These themes are still present in today's Native American literature, such as in the works of Duane Niatum, Gunn Allen, Louise Erdrich and N. Scott Momaday.

28. Oral debate is most closely associated with which form of discourse?

- A. Description
- B. Exposition
- C. Narration
- D. Persuasion

The answer is D. The purpose of a debate is to convince some audience or set of judges about something, which is very much the same as persuading some audience or set of judges about something.

29. Read the following passage:

"It would have been hard to find a passer-by more wretched in appearance. He was a man of middle height, stout and hardy, in the strength of maturity; he might have been forty-six or seven. A slouched leather cap hid half his face, bronzed by the sun and wind, and dripping with sweat."

What is its main form of discourse?

- A. Description
- B. Narration
- C. Exposition
- D. Persuasion

The answer is A. The passage describes the appearance of a person in detail. Narration tells a story. Exposition explains or informs. Persuasion promotes a point of view or course of action.

MIDDLE LEVEL ENGLISH

TEACHER CERTIFICATION EXAM

30. The arrangement and relationship of words in sentences or sentence structures best describes

    A. style.
    B. discourse.
    C. thesis.
    D. syntax.

The answer is D. Syntax is the grammatical structure of sentences. Style is not limited to considerations of syntax only, but includes vocabulary, voice, genre, and other language features. Discourse refers to investigating some idea. A thesis is a statement of opinion.

31. Identify the sentence that has an error in parallel structure.

    A. In order to help your favorite cause, you should contribute time or money, raise awareness, and write congressmen.
    B. Many people envision scientists working alone in a laboratory and discovering scientific breakthroughs.
    C. Some students prefer watching videos to textbooks because they are used to visual presentation.
    D. Tom Hanks, who has won two Academy Awards, is celebrated as an actor, director, and producer.

The answer is C. Parallel structure means that certain sentence structures in key positions match-up grammatically. In choice C, "watching videos" is a gerund phrase functioning as the direct object of the verb, and, because the verb implies a comparison, parallel construction requires that "textbooks" (functioning as the object of a currently-missing gerund) be preceded by an appropriate gerund--in this case, "reading." In order for the structure to be parallel, the sentence should read "Some students prefer <u>watching videos</u> to <u>*reading* textbooks</u> because they are used to visual presentation." They prefer something to something else. The other sentences conform to parallel structure. Recognizing parallel structure requires a sophisticated understanding of grammar.

MIDDLE LEVEL ENGLISH

TEACHER CERTIFICATION EXAM

32. Consider the following sentence:

Mr. Brown is a school volunteer <u>with a reputation and twenty years service</u>.

Which phrase below best represents the logical intent of the underlined phrase above? (Choice E is identical to the underlined phrase)

- A. with a reputation for twenty years' service
- B. with a reputation for twenty year's service
- C. who has served twenty years
- D. with a service reputation of twenty years

The correct answer is D. His reputation pertains to his service performance, not its duration. Choice A implies that it was for its duration. Choice B has Choice A's problem plus an incorrectly punctuated possessive. Choice C ignores his service reputation. Choice E is extremely vague.

33. Consider the following sentence:

Joe <u>didn't hardly know his cousin Fred</u>, who'd had a rhinoplasty.

Which word group below best conveys the intended meaning of the underlined section above?

- A. hardly did know his cousin Fred
- B. didn't know his cousin Fred hardly
- C. hardly knew his cousin Fred
- D. didn't know his cousin Fred

The correct answer is C. It contains a correctly-phrased negative expressed in the appropriate tense. Choice A has tense and awkwardness problems. Choice B has tense and double-negative problems. Choice D ignores the fact that he knew Fred a little. Choice E has tense and double-negative problems.

34. The literary device of personification is used in which example below?

   A. "Beg me no beggary by soul or parents, whining dog!"
   B. "Happiness sped through the halls cajoling as it went."
   C. "O wind thy horn, thou proud fellow."
   D. "And that one talent which is death to hide."

The correct answer is B. Personification is defined as giving human characteristics to inanimate objects or concepts. It can be thought of as a sub-category of metaphor. Happiness, an abstract concept, is "speeding through the halls" and "cajoling," both of which are human behaviors, so Happiness is being compared to a human being. Choice A is figurative and metaphorical, but not a personification. Choice C is, again, figurative and metaphorical, but not a personification. The speaker is, perhaps, telling someone that they are bragging, or "blowing their own horn." Choice D is also figurative and metaphorical, but not personification. Hiding a particular talent is being compared to risking death.

35. Among junior-high school students of low-to-average readability levels, which work would most likely stir reading interest?

   A. *Elmer Gantry*, Sinclair Lewis
   B. *Smiley's People*, John Le Carre
   C. *The Outsiders*, S.E. Hinton
   D. *And Then There Were None*, Agatha Christie.

The answer is C. The students can easily identify with the characters, the social issues, the vocabulary, and the themes in the book. The book deals with teenage concerns such as fitting-in, cliques, and appearance in ways that have proven very engaging for young readers.

TEACHER CERTIFICATION EXAM

36. Consider the following poem:

   My name is John Welington Wells,
   I'm a dealer in magic and spells,
   In blessings and curses,
   And ever-fill'd purses,
   In prophecies, witches, and knells.

   A. sonnet
   B. haiku
   C. limerick
   D. cinquain

The correct answer is C. A limerick is a five line, humorous verse, often nonsensical. with a rhyme scheme of aabba . Lines 1, 2, and 5 usually have eight syllables each; and lines 3 and 4 have five syllables. Line 5 is often some type of 'zinger.' A sonnet is a 14-line poem in iambic pentameter and having a definite rhyme scheme. Shakespearean and Petrarchan sonnets are the main varieties. A cinquain is a five-line poem with one word in line 1, two words in line 2, and so on through line 5.

37. Which of the following terms does *not* denote a figure of speech (figurative language)?

   A. Simile
   B. Euphemism
   C. Onomatopoeia
   D. Allusion

The answer is D. An allusion is an implied reference to a famous person, event, thing, or a part of another text. A simile is a direct comparison between two things. A euphemism is the substitution of an agreeable or inoffensive term for one that might offend. Onomatopoeia is vocal imitation to convey meaning—"bark" or "meow."

TEACHER CERTIFICATION EXAM

38. The first African American to receive the Pulitzer Prize for Poetry was

    A. Gwendolyn Brooks
    B. Harriet E. Wilson
    C. Richard Wright
    D. James Edwin Campbell

The correct answer is A. Gwendolyn Brooks was the first African American to receive the Pulitzer Prize for Poetry. Harriett E. Wilson, who died in 1900, was the first female African American novelist. Richard Wright was a novelist and black activist. James Edwin Campbell was a 19th century African American poet, editor, writer, and educator.

39. The principal writer of *The Declaration of Independence* was

    A. Patrick Henry
    B. Thomas Jefferson
    C. Ben Franklin
    D. George Washington

The correct answer is B. Thomas Jefferson. Although Benjamin Franklin was responsible for editing it and making it the prime example of neoclassical writing that it is, *The Declaration of Independence* came directly from the mind and pen of Jefferson. Patrick Henry was a great orator, and his speeches played an important role in precipitating the revolution. Although George Washington's *Farewell to the Army of the Potomac* is an important piece of writing from that era, he was not the principal writer of the declaration.

40. Pearl appears as an important character in

    A. *The Scarlet Letter*
    B. *Moby Dick*
    C. *The House of the Seven Gables*
    D. "The Cask of Amontillado"

The correct answer is A. Pearl is the illegitimate daughter of Hester Prynne in Nathaniel Hawthorne's *The Scarlet Letter*. *Moby Dick* is Herman Melville's great opus about the pursuit of a great white whale. *The House of the Seven Gables*, like *The Scarlet Letter,* is about a society that promulgates loneliness and suspicion. "The Cask of Amontillado" is one of Poe's horror stories.

TEACHER CERTIFICATION EXAM

41. The Old English period refers to

   A. The Fourth Century
   B. The Third through the Eighth Century
   C. The Fifth through the Tenth Century
   D. The Fifth through the Eighth Century

The correct answer is C. The Old English period begins with the settlement of the British Isles in the fifth and sixth centuries by Germanic tribes and continues until the time of Chaucer.

42. What factor below introduced Modern English?

   A. The Great Vowel Shift
   B. The printing press
   C. The invasion of the Normans
   D. Phonetic spelling

The correct answer is A. The Great Vowel Shift created guidelines for spelling and pronunciation in the wake of the invention of the printing press. Other answer choices, though related to the question, do not answer it as specifically.

43. Students are fluent readers if they

   A. read texts fast enough and with appropriate expression, or prosody.
   B. read word-to-word and haltingly.
   C. must intentionally decode a majority of the words.
   D. write disorganized sentences

The correct answer is A. A fluent reader reads words accurately, at target speeds, and with appropriate expression. It is a positive term. The other choices describe negative outcomes.

44. Reading assessment should take place

   A. At the end of the semester.
   B. At the end of a unit.
   C. Constantly.
   D. All of the above.

The correct answer is D. End-of-unit and end-of-semester measurements yield important information regarding achievement of course objectives and the evaluating of students' growth; however, assessment should be going on all the time so that the teacher can adjust instruction to meet the day-to-day needs of the students.

TEACHER CERTIFICATION EXAM

45. Effective assessment requires that

   A. Students not be involved in the assessment process.
   B. Testing activities are kept separate from the teaching activities.
   C. References materials that classroom instruction has prepared the students to read.
   D. Tests, in order to be reliable, should never use materials previously studied in the classroom

The correct answer is C. The only reliable measure of the success of a unit will be based on the reading the instruction has focused on. Choice A makes almost no sense; students will at the very least have to do something that can be assessed. Choice B calls into question the whole reason for schools. Choice D uses different phrases to accomplish the same unworthy end as Choice B.

46. Effective assessment means that

   A. It ignores age and cultural considerations
   B. Students' weaknesses are emphasized.
   C. Only reading skills count.
   D. It is integrated with instruction and is not intrusive.

The correct answer is D. Effective assessment informs instruction and practice. It is one phase of an integrated instructional cycle. Choice A ignores reality and distorts rather than informs. Choice B discourages students. Choice C ignores other important ways of demonstrating growth in understanding.

47. Which of the following approaches is *not* useful in assessing slower or immature readers?

   A. Repeated readings.
   B. Echo reading.
   C. Wide reading.
   D. Reading content that is more difficult than their skill levels in order to "stretch" their abilities.

The correct answer is D. Reading content for such students should be at a level where they can read and understand the word nuances, not at a level beyond such understanding and competence. Repeated readings of appropriate material builds this foundation. So does echo reading, or listening to a skilled reader and then trying to imitate his or her delivery. Wide reading is an approach intended to motivate students to read for pleasure and information from a variety of sources and involving socially-motivating processing routines.

TEACHER CERTIFICATION EXAM

48. A teacher should refer all of the following concerns to the appropriate expert except for

    A. Auditory trauma.
    B. Ear infection.
    C. Vision problems.
    D. Underdeveloped vocabulary.

The answer is D. The teacher is the expert in vocabulary development. The other choices require a medical professional.

49. Middle-School students bring little, if any, initial experience in

    A. Phonics.
    B. Phonemics.
    C. Textbook reading assignments.
    D. Stories read by the teacher.

The correct answer is C. In middle school, probably for the first time, the student will be expected to read textbook assignments and come to class prepared to discuss the content. Students get phonics (the systematic study of decoding) in the early grades, and they normally get phonemics (familiarity with the syllable sounds of English) even earlier. They will have almost certainly had stories read to them by a teacher by the time they get to middle school.

50. To enhance reading comprehension, experts recommend all of these techniques except for

    A. Read material through only once, but read slowly and carefully.
    B. Read material through more than once according to a plan.
    C. Create a map for the next reading.
    D. Highlight or take notes during reading.

The correct answer is A. While reading at a rate that assures accuracy is desirable, there is no evidence to support a recommendation to avoid rereading something. Choice B is advisable because it proposes a purpose for the rereadings. Choice C is advisable because it also addresses purpose. Choice D is advisable because it helps students maintain focus as they read.

TEACHER CERTIFICATION EXAM

51. In the hierarchy of needs for adolescents who are becoming more team-oriented in their approach to learning, which need do they exhibit most?

    A. Need for competence
    B. Need for love/acceptance
    C. Need to know
    D. Need to belong

The answer is B. Abraham's Maslow's theory of Humanistic Development that such older children and adolescents exhibit most a need for love/acceptance from peers and potential romantic partners. Their need for competence is in the service of gaining the love/acceptance. Their need to know is developing, but is not their primary issue. Their need to belong does not address their emerging sexual identities.

52. What is the best course of action when a child refuses to complete an assignment on the ground that is morally objectionable?

    A. Speak with the parents and explain the necessity of studying this work.
    B. Encourage the child to sample some of the text before making a judgment.
    C. Place the child in another teacher's class where students are studying an acceptable work.
    D. Provide the student with alternative material that serves the same curricular purpose.

The answer is D. This approach is the most time efficient and flexible. Choice A requires conversations involving value systems that aren't going to change. Choice B risks being open to the charge of exposing children to controversial material despite parental input. Choice C is a disproportionate disruption to the student's schedule and the school routine.

TEACHER CERTIFICATION EXAM

53. **Which of the following responses to literature typically give middle school students the most problems?**

    A. Interpretive
    B. Evaluative
    C. Critical
    D. Emotional

The answer is B. Middle school readers will exhibit both emotional and interpretive responses. In middle/junior high school, organized study models enable students to identify main ideas and supporting details, to recognize sequential order, to distinguish fact from opinion, and to determine cause/effect relationships. Middle school students can provide reasons to support their assertions that a particular book was boring or a particular poem made him or her feel sad, and this is to provide a critical reaction on a fundamental level. Evaluative responses, however, require students to address how the piece represents its genre, how well it reflects the social and ethical mores of a given society, or how well the author has employed a fresh approach to the subject. Evaluative responses are more sophisticated than critical responses, and they are appropriate for advanced high school students.

54. **Overcrowded classes prevent the individual attention needed to facilitate language development. This drawback can be best overcome by**

    A. Dividing the class into independent study groups.
    B. Assigning more study time at home.
    C. Using more drill practice in class.
    D. Team teaching.

The answer is A. Dividing a class into small groups maximizes opportunities for engagement. Assigning more study time at home is passing the buck. Using more drill practice in class is likely to bore most students to tears. Team teaching begs the question; if you can get another teacher, then your class should no longer be overcrowded.

TEACHER CERTIFICATION EXAM

55. **The most significant drawback to applying learning theory research to classroom practice is that**

    A. today's students do not acquire reading skills with the same alacrity as when greater emphasis was placed on reading classical literature.
    B. development rates are complicated by geographical and cultural differences that are difficult to overcome.
    C. homogeneous grouping has contributed to faster development of some age groups.
    D. social and environmental conditions have contributed to an escalated maturity level than research done twenty or more years ago would seem to indicate.

The answer is D. A mismatch exists between what interests today's students and the learning materials presented to them. Choice A is a significant problem only if the school insists on using classical literature exclusively. Choice B does describe a drawback, but students are more alike in their disengagement from anachronistic learning materials than they are different due to their culture and geographical location. Choice C describes a situation that is not widespread.

56. **Modeling is a practice that requires students to**

    A. create a style unique to their own language capabilities.
    B. emulate the writing of professionals.
    C. paraphrase passages from good literature.
    D. peer evaluate the writings of other students.

The answer is B. Modeling engages students in analyzing the writing of professional writers and in imitating the syntactical, grammatical and stylistic mastery of that writer. Choice A is an issue of voice. Choice C is a less rigorous form of the correct answer. Choice D is only very indirectly related to modeling.

TEACHER CERTIFICATION EXAM

57. Reading a piece of student writing to assess the overall impression of the product is

   A. holistic evaluation.
   B. portfolio assessment.
   C. analytical evaluation.
   D. using a performance system.

The answer is A. In holistic scoring, the teacher reads quickly through a paper once to get a general impression and assigns a rating based on a rubric that includes the criteria for achievement in a few, key dimensions of the assignment. Portfolio assessment involves tracking work over stages or over time. Analytical evaluation involves breaking down the assignment into discrete traits and determining achievement in each of those traits. A performance system refers to engaging students in writing assignments meant to generate products in a given time frame. Often, such products are scored holistically.

58. A formative evaluation of student writing

   A. requires a thorough marking of mechanical errors with a pencil or pen.
   B. makes comments on the appropriateness of the student's interpretation of the prompt and the degree to which the objective was met.
   C. requires the student to hand in all the materials produced during the process of writing.
   D. involves several careful readings of the text for content, mechanics, spelling, and usage.

The answer is B. Formative evaluations should support the students' writing process through strategic feedback at key points. Teacher comments and feedback should encourage recursive revision and metacognition. Choice A applies, if anywhere, to a summative evaluation of student writing. Choice C is a neutral management strategy. A teacher can make formative evaluations without collecting all the materials. Choice D, again, is more suited for summative evaluation or for the very last issue in the composition process, namely proofreading.

59. Writing ideas quickly without interruption of the flow of thoughts or attention to conventions is called

   A. brainstorming.
   B. mapping.
   C. listing.
   D. Free writing.

The answer is D. Free writing is a particular type of brainstorming (techniques to generate ideas). Mapping is another type and results in products resembling flow charts. Listing is another brainstorming technique that differs from free writing in that free writing is more open-ended and looks more like sentences.

60. The students in Mrs. Cline's seventh grade language arts class were invited to attend a performance of *Romeo and Juliet* presented by the drama class at the high school. To best prepare, they should

   A. read the play as a homework exercise.
   B. read a synopsis of the plot and a biographical sketch of the author.
   C. examine a few main selections from the play to become familiar with the language and style of the author.
   D. read a condensed version of the story and practice attentive listening skills.

The answer is D. By reading a condensed version of the play, students will know the plot and therefore be better able to follow the play on stage. They will also practice being attentive. Choice A is far less dynamic and few will do it. Choice B is likewise dull. Choice C is not thorough enough.

61. Which of the following sentences is unambiguously properly punctuated?

   A. The more you eat; the more you want.
   B. The authors—John Steinbeck, Ernest Hemingway, and William Faulkner—are staples of modern writing in American literature textbooks.
   C. Handling a wild horse, takes a great deal of skill and patience
   D. The man, who replaced our teacher, is a comedian.

The answer is B. Dashes should be used instead of commas when commas are used elsewhere in the sentence for amplification or explanation—here within the dashes. Choice A has a semicolon where there should be a comma. Choice C has a comma that shouldn't be there at all. Choice D could be correct in a non-restrictive context, and so whether or not it is correct is ambiguous.

62. In a timed essay test of an hour's duration, how much time should be devoted to prewriting.

   A. five
   B. ten
   C. fifteen
   D. twenty

The answer is B. Ten minutes of careful planning still allows sufficient time for the other stages of the writing process. Five minutes would result more dead-ends and backtracking. Fifteen and twenty minutes would result in rushing drafting, revising, and editing.

63. A student informative composition should consist of a minimum of how many paragraphs?

   A. three
   B. four
   C. five
   D. six

The answer is C. This composition would consist of an introductory paragraph, three body paragraphs, and a concluding paragraph. A three or four paragraph composition could include all three types of paragraphs, but would not require the students to elaborate at sufficient length in the body of the paper. A six paragraph minimum is slightly excessive, more or less by tradition.

64. In 'inverted triangle' introductory paragraphs, the thesis sentence occurs

   A. at the beginning of the paragraph.
   B. in the middle of the paragraph.
   C. at the end of the paragraph.
   D. in the second paragraph.

The answer is C. The beginning of the paragraph should establish interest, the middle of the paragraph should establish a general context, and the paragraph should end with the thesis that the rest of the paper will develop. Delaying the thesis until the second paragraph would be 'outside the triangle.'

65. A punctuation mark indicating omission, interrupted thought, or an incomplete statement is a/an

- A. ellipsis.
- B. anachronism.
- C. colloquy.
- D. idiom.

The answer is A. In an ellipsis, a word or words that would clarify the sentence's message are missing, yet it is still possible to understand them from the context. An anachronism is something out of its proper time frame. A colloquy is a formal conversation or dialogue. An idiom is a saying peculiar to some language group.

66. Which of the following would be the most significant factor in teaching Homer's *Iliad* and *Odyssey* to any particular group of students?

- A. Identifying a translation on the appropriate reading level
- B. Determining the student's interest level
- C. Selecting an appropriate evaluative technique
- D. Determining the scope and delivery methods of background study

The answer is A. Students will appreciate these two works if the translation reflects both the vocabulary they know and their reading level. Choice B is moot because most students aren't initially interested in Homer. Choice C skips to later matters. Choice D is tempting and significant, but not as crucial as having an accessible text.

67. Which of the following contains an error in possessive punctuation?

- A. Doris's shawl
- B. mother's-in-law frown
- C. children's lunches
- D. ambassador's briefcase

The answer is B. Mother-in-law is a compound common noun, and the apostrophe should come at the end of the word, according to convention. The other choices are correctly punctuated.

TEACHER CERTIFICATION EXAM

68. Which aspect of language is innate?

   A. Biological capability to articulate sounds understood by other humans
   B. Cognitive ability to create syntactical structures
   C. Capacity for using semantics to convey meaning in a social environment
   D. Ability to vary inflections and accents

The answer is A. The biological capability to articulate sounds understood by other humans is innate; and, later, children learn semantics and syntactical structures through trial and error. Linguists agree that language is first a vocal system of word symbols that enable a human to communicate his or her feelings, thoughts, and desires to other human beings.

69. Written on the sixth grade reading level, most of S. E. Hinton's novels (for instance, *The Outsiders*) have the greatest reader appeal with

   A. sixth graders.
   B. ninth graders.
   C. twelfth graders.
   D. adults.

The answer is B. Adolescents are concerned with their changing bodies, their relationships with each other and adults, and their place in society. Reading *The Outsiders* helps them confront different problems that they are only now beginning to experience as teenagers, such as gangs and social identity. The book is universal in its appeal to adolescents.

70. After watching a movie of a train derailment, a child exclaims, "Wow, look how many cars fell off the tracks. There's junk everywhere. The engineer must have really been asleep." Using the facts that the child is impressed by the wreckage and assigns blame to the engineer, a follower of Piaget's theories would estimate the child to be about

   A. ten years old.
   B. twelve years old.
   C. fourteen years old.
   D. sixteen years old.

The answer is A. According to Piaget's theory, children seven to eleven years old begin to apply logic to concrete things and experiences. They can combine performance and reasoning to solve problems. They have internalized moral values and are willing to confront rules and adult authority.

MIDDLE LEVEL ENGLISH

TEACHER CERTIFICATION EXAM

71. **Which of the following should not be included in the opening paragraph of an informative essay?**

    A. Thesis sentence
    B. Details and examples supporting the main idea
    C. broad general introduction to the topic
    D. A style and tone that grabs the reader's attention

The answer is B. The introductory paragraph should introduce the topic, capture the reader's interest, state the thesis and prepare the reader for the main points in the essay. Details and examples, however, belong in the second part of the essay, the body paragraphs.

72. **Children's literature became established in the**

    A. seventeenth century
    B. eighteenth century
    C. nineteenth century
    D. twentieth century

The answer is A. In the seventeenth century, Jean de la Fontaine's *Fables*, Pierre Perreault's *Tales*, Mme. d'Aulnoye's novels based on old folktales, and Mme. de Beaumont's *Beauty and the Beast* created a children's literature genre. In England, Perreault was translated, and a work allegedly written by Oliver Smith, *The Renowned History of Little Goody Two Shoes*, helped to establish children's literature in England, too.

73. **Which of the following is the least effective procedure for promoting consciousness of audience?**

    A. Pairing students during the writing process
    B. Reading all rough drafts before the students write the final copies
    C. Having students compose stories or articles for publication in school literary magazines or newspapers
    D. Writing letters to friends or relatives

The answer is B. Reading all rough drafts will do the least to promote consciousness of audience; they are very used to turning papers into the teacher, and most don't think much about impressing the teacher. Pairing students will ensure a small, constant audience about whom they care; and having them compose stories for literary magazines will encourage them to put their best efforts forward because their work will be read by an actual audience in an impressive format. Writing letters also engages students in thinking about how best to communicate with a particular audience.

MIDDLE LEVEL ENGLISH

TEACHER CERTIFICATION EXAM

74. Which of the following is not a technique of prewriting?

　　A. Clustering
　　B. Listing
　　C. Brainstorming
　　D. Proofreading

The answer is D. You cannot proofread something that you have not yet written. While it is true that prewriting involves written techniques, prewriting is not concerned with punctuation, capitalization, and spelling (proofreading). Brainstorming is a general term denoting generating ideas, and clustering and listing are specific methods of brainstorming.

XAMonline, INC. 21 Orient Ave. Melrose, MA 02176
Toll Free number 800-509-4128
TO ORDER Fax 781-662-9268 OR www.XAMonline.com

CERTIFICATION EXAMINATION FOR OKLAHOMA EDUCATORS - CEOE - 2007

PO#   Store/School:

Address 1:

Address 2 (Ship to other):
City, State Zip

Credit card number _____-_____-_____-_____   expiration _____
EMAIL _____
PHONE   **FAX**

13# ISBN 2007	TITLE	Qty	Retail	Total
978-1-58197-781-3	CEOE OSAT Advanced Mathematics Field 11			
978-1-58197-775-2	CEOE OSAT Art Sample Test Field 02			
978-1-58197-780-6	CEOE OSAT Biological Sciences Field 10			
978-1-58197-776-9	CEOE OSAT Chemistry Field 04			
978-1-58197-778-3	CEOE OSAT Earth Science Field 08			
978-1-58197-794-3	CEOE OSAT Elementary Education Fields 50-51			
978-1-58197-795-0	CEOE OSAT Elementary Education Fields 50-51 Sample Questions			
978-1-58197-777-6	CEOE OSAT English Field 07			
978-1-58197-779-0	CEOE OSAT Family and Consumer Sciences Field 09			
978-1-58197-786-8	CEOE OSAT French Sample Test Field 20			
978-1-58197-798-1	CEOE OGET Oklahoma General Education Test 074			
978-1-58197-792-9	CEOE OSAT Library-Media Specialist Field 38			
978-1-58197-787-5	CEOE OSAT Middle Level English Field 24			
978-1-58197-789-9	CEOE OSAT Middle Level Science Field 26			
978-1-58197-790-5	CEOE OSAT Middle Level Social Studies Field 27			
978-1-58197-788-2	CEOE OSAT Middle Level-Intermediate Mathematics Field 25			
978-1-58197-791-2	CEOE OSAT Mild Moderate Disabilities Field 29			
978-1-58197-782-0	CEOE OSAT Physical Education-Health-Safety Field 12			
978-1-58197-783-7	CEOE OSAT Physics Sample Test Field 14			
978-1-58197-793-6	CEOE OSAT Principal Common Core Field 44			
978-1-58197-796-7	CEOE OPTE Oklahoma Professional Teaching Examination Fields 75-76			
978-1-58197-784-4	CEOE OSAT Reading Specialist Field 15			
978-1-58197-785-1	CEOE OSAT Spanish Field 19			
978-1-58197-797-4	CEOE OSAT U.S. & World History Field 17			
			SUBTOTAL	
FOR PRODUCT PRICES GO TO WWW.XAMONLINE.COM			Ship	$8.25
			TOTAL	

www.ingramcontent.com/pod-product-compliance
Lightning Source LLC
Chambersburg PA
CBHW080539300426
44111CB00017B/2794